To Maurice

For Your Birthday

July 19 1997

With lots of love

from

Ivy & Glenn.

x

# Cookham

## Its Birds, People & Places.

# The Contributors

*Bill & Jackie Beglow*

*Philip & Marie-Thérèse Ind*

*Anne Keating*

*Brian & Hazel Clews*

*Doll & Claire Cooper &
May Godfrey*

*Martin & Shirley Gostling*

*Jeremy & Tina Langham*

# Cookham
## Its Birds, People and Places.

A walk through the village, and its past.

by
**BRIAN CLEWS**

**BCS**

Published by
BCS, 118 Broomhill, Cookham, Berkshire SL6 9LQ
© Brian D. Clews 1996

ISBN 0 9529248 0 3

Set in Bell 11pt
and printed by

WILLOW PRESS
Bourton-on-the-Water
Gloucestershire
01451 820231

# Foreword

MANY OF US KNOW the joys of walking around the village of Cookham and how such walks can be enhanced by a knowledgeable friend to point out landmarks and points of interest. In this book, Brian Clews gives us the opportunity to have our walks illuminated by his observations, not only of the places and people of our village, but also the rich bird-life which surrounds us. Those of us who are yet to be awakened to an understanding of ornithology will want to keep this book as a constant companion to enhance our appreciation of this beautiful corner of Berkshire. As for those already versed in this fascinating field, they will appreciate the careful attention to detail.

All who know Cookham will enjoy this extremely readable account of life in our village as we move towards the end of this century, and Brian Clews will take his place alongside Darby, the Bootles, Roger Parkes and Luke Over, in preserving our history for future generations to enjoy.

Father David Rossdale<br>
Holy Trinity, Cookham.

# The Contributors

*Peter & Irene Gaines*

*David & Sue Wright*

*Martin Britnell*

*John Turk*

*John Field*

*John & Bridie Webb + Olivia Chapman*

# Acknowledgements

I INITIALLY WANTED to bring up to date the observations of W H Hudson who, a century ago, recorded the status of numerous species of birds in our village. Indeed, it was to be called *Birds In Our Village*. However, in researching people's recollections of the changing fortunes of birds in a developing Cookham, more needed to be said about the people themselves, and about the walks they have discovered over the years. The consequent re-direction and change of title has resulted in what follows. No work of this nature is possible without the valuable help and contribution of a number of people. That certainly became the case with this book.

Firstly, thanks are due to all those photographed opposite for their permission to give a snap shot of their life and recollections of the Cookhams. Many of them did not know me before I 'descended' upon them and I greatly appreciate their support. Any inaccuracy in historic fact is more likely to be due to my note-taking than their memory of times gone past.

Then there are those who contributed illustrations to the book. The full detail appears in the appendices, but I particularly want to thank Barbara Pritchard for many of the bird drawings, David Wright for sketches of buildings, David Colthup for the cover line drawing and my sister Barbara Clews for the coloured drawings on the jacket. My friend Martin Gostling spent much time entering the drawings and photographs.

Another friend, David White, carried out valuable research on some of the family names of the last century and I am also indebted to Lynda Whitworth for her willingness to carry out the difficult task of proof reading. I was amazed that Father David Rossdale found enough time to read the book and provide a foreword in the midst of a busy Parish to run.

I am grateful to those who subscribed to the production of the book, and who are listed in the appendices. Finally, I need to say a big 'thank you' to my most tolerant wife, Hazel. Born and bred in the village, she was very supportive in my task, but there was many a paint job, loose screw or clearing up task that never got dealt with whilst I was busy on the keyboard.

# Introduction

Can there be a nicer place to live than the Cookhams? But how many of us make the time to get to know it well; to explore its hidden corners and to consider its wildlife. As a keen birdwatcher, I have found that there is a richness of birdlife in the Cookhams that most likely goes un-noticed for many of us. In this book, I hope to enlighten and enthuse you about this side of life in Cookham.

Others may well have written about the birds of Cookham but not for a long time; indeed, W H Hudson's book *Birds in a Village* seems to have been the only one I can trace and that celebrates its 100th anniversary this year. Time perhaps to bring Hudson's findings up to date.

Much has been recorded about the history of the village, its prominent founders and its buildings of historic interest, in such exactitude as warrants no restating. But the more recent history is less well recorded and many family names, some present for generations, are also less well recorded for the benefit of future historians. In taking a snap-shot of the village in the nineties, and recording some people's reminiscences going back several decades, I hope future generations will find something useful to aid their exploration of family history.

Memories of trades and shops are fading. An appendix of such businesses as exist in 1996 is included to help future historians. There have been many shops and traders lost to the village in recent years due to the competition of larger supermarkets in the area; a lesson for us to remember to support our local shops if we do not want to lose the advantages they provide us and their role in maintaining village life.

Cookham, along with the rest of the world, is just about to step into the uncertainties of not just a new century, but a new millennium. Has our past prepared us for the future? Have the lives of our forebears provided a foundation from which we step into the future, or are their experiences irrelevant to us? I prefer to think not. The fascination of one generation for its history and background is a healthy way of staying rooted in reality and reaching an understanding of why things are the way they are. A generation severed from its past will risk free-wheeling without direction into the same problems encountered in a previous era and there will be no progress. New thinking tells us that only the 'now' and the 'future' matter, but I believe we ignore the past at our peril. God gives us past by which we might steer our tomorrows, and He expects us to value the former things as He does.

It is intended that some of the proceeds of this book will go towards the running of Cookham Day Centre at Elizabeth House. By this small means, those who have striven to fashion our past and propel us into the future might be recognised and honoured by the present generation, as a token of gratitude and a symbol of our wishes for their well-being.

Therefore, if you know someone who hasn't bought this book yet, please bully them into doing so!

*Elizabeth House*

JANUARY
  Brightness, dullness, frost and rain,
  January's come again.
  Leading time in ordained fashion,
  Refreshing hearts in yearly passion.

    Hordes of Pigeon make grey the tree-tops,
    Swoop in gangs to stomp the crops.
    'Tu-Wits' demand their 'Hoo-Hoo' answer,
    Whilst Partridge vie for 'best dawn dancer'.

# BIRDLIFE IN COOKHAM

A CENTURY OR SO AGO, Cookham was a different place. Hardly a profound statement perhaps, but the changes that have taken place during the last century have affected the local avifauna in many ways. In their book, *The Story of Cookham*, Robin and Valerie Bootle give us pictures of Cookham at different times over the centuries. Some 130 years ago, the present village was the centre of social and trading activity, serving a busy travelling route and an active river industry. Hospitality and hard work grew up together side by side with 16 pubs and beer cellars to serve 700 families. The 12th century church was the centre of the community and the 'new' church of St John the Baptist had only just been constructed. This was necessary because of "desecration of the Holy Day of rest. Hereditary Sabbath-breaking has prevailed in this place, descending from parents to children and has led to the lowest level of ignorance and vice" according to the vicar of Cookham in 1844. The pond in Kings Lane, aptly named Deadman's Pond, was eventually filled following the drowning of Dick Hatch, whose body was discovered by my wife's uncle, Jim Skinner.

The recently-opened railway station had started bringing even more people and business to the area, but beyond the station to the north and west, where now lies Cookham Rise, were extensive commons and farmland. Cockmarsh and Widbrook were probably more marshy than they are now and gamekeepers strutted around performing their gun-toting errands for the landed gentry.

It was of this form of Cookham that Alexander W M Clark Kennedy wrote about in 1868 when he penned his *Birds of Berkshire and Buckinghamshire*. He went on to join the Coldstream Guards and eventually became a JP for Kircudbrightshire, then Dumfriesshire and eventually Dorset. However, during his time as a student at Eton, he was determined to study the bird-life of our region, resulting in what was probably the first recorded status of many of the species that frequented our locality in those halcyon days. His studies at Eton prevented extensive personal survey but, no doubt through friends of his moneyed parents, he was able to commission many a gamekeeper to submit information about birds both rare and common.

Unfortunately, in those days, there were few guide books to aid recognition and only rudimentary field glasses or telescopes. The only way an observer could ensure a positive identification for the less common species was to shoot it and take its carcass to an expert. This did little for the fortunes of rarer birds which obviously became even rarer! No doubt too, with no such thing as 24 hour Parcel Force, there would have been interesting aromas permeating the corridors of learning as yet another challenge to Kennedy's prowess in identification was carefully unpacked.

Ornithologists in that bygone era would have thrilled at finding Little Bittern breeding on the Thames towards Maidenhead, as occurred in 1826, Harriers would have regularly quartered the farmland around us, a Marsh Harrier being shot near Cockmarsh in 1881. A Great Snipe found favour in the relative wilderness in 1860 and Stone Curlew, with their gangly knees and staring ET-like eyes, would have been a common sight in fields embracing the Chiltern escarpment. Sufficient river-side reeds attracted Bearded Tits and Dartford Warblers churred on surrounding commons.

Born in Argentina, the well-known ornithologist and wildlife expert W H Hudson came to our shores in 1869. Looking for a perfect rural setting to write about village birds, he selected Cookham and stayed for two summer months at the end of the last century. He was enthralled with 59 species which became the subject of his book *'Birds of a Village'*. Captivated by Nightingales and Wrynecks, and the charm of the village itself, his book portrays an appreciation of all the things, bright and beautiful, about Cookham. Small wonder that Clark Kennedy wrote in his own preface: "While the world endures, be it a thousand years or a million of centuries, the works of God will never be fully comprehended by man; and there is delightful occupation in view for all time."

An even earlier view on Berkshire in spring came from another Eton intern; Sir Henry Wotton, Provost of Eton c1650 who wrote of a Berkshire springtime;

> *"This Day dame Nature seem'd in love:*
> *The lusty sap began to move;*
> *Fresh juice did stir th' embracing vines;*
> *And birds had drawn their Valentines."*

In Cookham itself, Alice Ray Morton's 'granny', Bess, well recalled *"the Corncrakes, so noisy of an evening from the croplands, all but shot off.*

*The night-time purring of the eve-jar (Nightjar) gone from the thickets. The Kingfishers getting so rare when once you'd never see less than a dozen in an hours walk along the water. Great flocks of wildfowl along the river, less and less on the wing, the Herons and Curlew too."* We can sit with our eyes closed, imagining the sights and sounds of that hay-time scene, the Moor without cars and ice-cream vans. The roar of the traffic replaced with the honking of the geese. The occasional 'tourist' in a horse-drawn coach instead of the hoards of motorised moochers of today. The hiss of the twice-daily steam train compared to the roar of the twice-minutely jet from Heathrow. Yes, we can do that; or we can go in search of what Cookham still has to offer. You see, whilst the world about has gone mad for activity, noise, speed and the like, Cookham has kept hidden an aura of the past in its cupboard of tranquillity. Corners where tempus has been refused permission to fugit and where essences of its youth reside in a spice rack of time.

You know, I often see folk just strolling along, or walking the doggie, totally oblivious of what is happening around them, or worse still, jogging through the lanes as if to ensure no spectacle of nature impairs their day. A visiting spectator wrote in 1893; "The villager is, as a rule, not a good observer". What a shame! So much to see and such embellishment available for every outing. This is particularly so of our birds. Oh yes, our plant-life is beautiful, but plants don't move or talk to us, even if we talk to them! Butterflies too are gloriously coloured and move around evocatively, but they don't make a sound either and are only present in summer. Only our wild birds can appeal to our senses of sight and hearing and fascinate us with their lifestyle, all year round. When we examine them closely, we find them to be examples of extravagant creation. Few other creatures exhibit such satisfaction in being provided for our pleasure.

So, why not join me on a walk that goes backwards and forwards through time, reflecting on these changes in the eyes of the birds, and some of the people. Let's set off, with no need to rush, taking a little time to stand and stare, and don't forget your bins! If you do not possess a pair, perhaps borrow some from a friend, or better still, drag your friend out with you. Failing that, forego the next dinner outing and spend the money saved on a pair for yourself. (8x30's or 10x50's are best). Where better to start than the cricket pitch in Whyteladyes Lane.

# Bowling Along

The pitch was created on land donated by Jim Rickets in 1983, whereas the club hut itself was a disused building from Moor Hall, painstakingly dismantled and rebuilt, opening in May 1984. The pitch in season is be-decked with scampering figures in ghostly white apparel. So it was 50 or more years ago when a young Mrs Godfrey recounted the great 'White Owls' which frequented the fields behind her house in Whyteladyes Lane. Walking 'The Kennels', Mrs Godfrey would often espy these silent hunters quartering the meadow in search of a tasty vole or field mouse, and indeed they would have been relatively common at that time, before the increase of insecticide devastated their numbers nation-wide.

In later years, with pram in tow, Mrs Godfrey would have walked the same path with no Barn Owl in sight. However, there is an exciting possibility that a re-introduction scheme might be undertaken in the area. Roger Parkes, who has lived in Cartlands Cottage with his wife Tessa for some 25 years, and is the author of 'Alice Ray Morton's Cookham', is a keen ornithologist with a determination to see the Barn Owl restored to Cookham. Cartlands was built around 300 years ago, and is believed to be named after one John Cartland whose name appears in the constables notebook of 1840 as having been indicted for murder! With fond memories of village birds seen whilst walking Dusty, the family goat, Roger recalls the Redshank that once nested on Cockmarsh, the many Kingfishers that frequented the area, and the 'Memorable Birding Moment' when a Hobby first appeared near the cottage. Whilst unable to bring back the Redshanks, Roger is determined to improve the fortunes of our 'White Owl', so we might still see this magnificent creature once again in its rightful place, just beyond square leg! Oh, and the contents of the aforementioned pram? Her name was Hazel and she is now my wife!

But now, the pampered green is a feeding station for many a Pied Wagtail, summer and winter alike as it is a resident species, not taken to intercontinental holidaying. The adults are striking in their black and white plumage, constantly on the move and tail wagging more than a terrier at home-coming. Their little bodies on a long 'handle' resulted in its local name of 'Dishwasher'. Have you ever noticed the different ways small birds traverse the ground? This one is a twinkle-footed runner, rather than a hopper. In summer, numerous juveniles turn out for their trial on the hallowed patch, but seem rarely selected, disappearing by late autumn. Skylarks feed from the Bradcutts Lane end whilst Linnets favour the spectators enclosure, ensuring a quick getaway to the fir trees nearby. These same trees have hosted a family of Whitethroats in some years, their distinctive white chins and grey heads marking them out from the other 'little brown jobs' that play along the lane. Much more a bird of heaths and commons, the Whitethroat has adapted well to the onset of farmland and mature gardens, particularly in corners that have any sense of 'wildness' about them.

A bird of extremes, the Whitethroat. It's either lurking in the depths of a briar churring and chacking in disgust at your presence, thoroughly earning its medieval nick-name 'Churr Muffit', or sitting atop a prominent perch issuing its scratchy, descending song which seems to say ♪ "I wish you all the joy I have" ♪. Then next it might leap up with a flourish, jerking and clambering up an invisible spiral staircase, only to flutter exaggeratingly downwards again in full song. Such a showy performance can, of course, only belong to a male, endeavouring to impress any of the opposite gender in the vicinity.

Turning about, we see the great prairie fields leading down to Lower Mount farm, and beyond to Canon Court, with the miscellany of housing styles that have erupted along Whyteladyes Lane. The ancient hedgerows and tree-lines that once segmented Cookham's farmland have long since been 'cleansed' from the scene, to 'make it easier to move farm plant from one part of the farm to another'. Strange, however, that the *roads* still reverberate with tractor, baler and harvester alike. Still, that's

*Pied Wagtail*

perhaps the cost of living in a little bit of Heaven. This whole area included much common land a hundred years ago "where it was possible to spend an hour or two without seeing a human creature, in this paradise of birds" as W H Hudson described it. Nowadays, the fields are rotated by crop, affecting the species of bird likely to be encountered, but Skylarks and Meadow Pipits abound in winter, often together on the ground, never together in the air. The Pipit often seems to be flying two strokes forward and one back, as if suffering intermittent mis-fires, or faulty petrol, its high pitched call further confirming its frustrated action.

No such limitations on the Lark. Straight into the aerial elevator, press the button marked 'cloud level' and it seems instantly there. From this vantage point, it proceeds to pour liquid silver into the atmosphere, its incessant tune uplifting any mood. Often, it proves impossible to actually see where this speckled speck is singing from, like some invisible tape player in the skies. And if an Exaltation of Larks are singing in unison, it's like a Royal Variety Performance. No wonder Wordsworth called the Skylark 'the pilgrim of the sky'. And of this champion of song Izaac Walton wrote *"At first the Lark, when she means to rejoyce, to chear herself up and those that hear her, she then quits the earth, and sings as she ascends higher into the air, and having ended her Heavenly employment, grows then mute and sad to think she must descend to the sad earth, which she would not touch, but for necessity."*

Wordsworth could not restrain himself from recording his own appreciation:

*Up with me! Up with me into the clouds!*
*For thy song, Lark, is strong;*
*Up with me, up with me into the clouds!*
*Singing, singing,*
*With clouds and sky above thee ringing,*
*Lift me, guide me till I find*
*That spot which seems so to thy mind.*

Shelley added his praise of this aerial master in his ode to the Skylark;

*Hail to thee, blithe spirit!*
*Bird thou never wert -*
*That from heaven or near it*
*Pourest thy full heart*
*In profuse strains of unpremeditated art.*

Indeed, if you listen closely, it can be discerned that this is a song not written on a score, but is delicately improvised from practised phrases enjoined as lacework on the air. Usually the song is in fairly lengthy bursts of several seconds, but they can go for up to 5 minutes without a break, and this whilst maintaining station on constant flapping wings. Have you ever heard one sounding out of breath? Try timing one sometime.

Farming practices have changed dramatically in recent years, affecting many bird species. Double cropping, margin clearance and the replacement of hedges with lovely looking wire fences have put our traditional farmland species under great pressure. There are three million fewer Skylarks now than twenty years ago, for example. Another species which has suffered perhaps a more marked decline than most is the Corn Bunting. As its name suggests, it prospers best in corn or barley crops, nesting in the margins and relying on minimum disturbance during fledging time. Mr E M Nicholson, a Deanite in the 20's, records Corn Buntings as "only observed during summer in the Dean" in his notes of 1926. Since then, numbers have crashed throughout the country, but Cookhamites are lucky. A very small remnant can sometimes be found around the fields behind Whyteladyes Lane, usually detected by the birds peculiar but delightful metallic, jingling call, uttered from fence-lines or tree tops. If close enough, or using bins, the huge gape of this big-billed bunting can be clearly seen as it rattles its car keys at all who will listen.

A temporary reprieve has been granted in the form of farmland set-aside, a means of reducing over production of crops recompensed by government grants. These areas have proven invaluable for ground nesting species and farmer Copas has aided a change in the mowing times set by the Ministry - further helping the tenuous grip the Corn Bunting has in the county. This bulky Bunting, with its striated chest and sized between a Spug and a Song Thrush, used to be known as the Corn Dumpling, which I think is a far better name.

---

## FEBRUARY

Second in the given order
Hints of life in many border.
Interminable nights and fleeting days,
A spring to come, for which give praise.

       Gulls on the common in silver parade
       Squadrons of Starlings the roof-tops invade.
       Noble Fieldfares spie the hip,
       Whilst Meadow Pipits hail Sip! Sip! Sip!

It is another essential piece in the jigsaw of Cookham's past and present. I'm not too sure of the future, though. One must hope that it does not suffer the demise of it's kinsman, the Cirl Bunting. Recorded "in treetops in Cookham" in June 1924 by the aforementioned Mr Nicholson, the species survives now in only a few Cornish and Devonian meadows.

A keen member of the Cookham Cricket Club Supporters is Jeremy Langham who has lived in Gorse Rd in the Rise with his wife Tina since 1989, having met at the Met Office in Bracknell where they both worked. Jeremy is also leader of the East Berkshire Group of the Royal Society for the Protection of Birds, a task he has performed since 1976 when he was appointed Local Representative. A keen birdwatcher since 1967, when he was just 9 years old, Jeremy has led many a local bird-watching walk and always enjoys his encounters with Cookham's Little Owls, and the Siskins which visit us in winter. In fact, his most 'Memorable Birding Moment' was finding a somewhat disorientated Little Owl sitting in the middle of the road near Widbrook at 5.30am one morning. Picking up this ball of feathers, he placed it safely in a hedge. Later in the morning he rang Tina who collected it and took it to Joan Grant who lived in the Old Court Hotel at Boulters Lock. Joan had a reputation for caring for injured birds and she soon resuscitated the dazed owl. Jeremy misses the Barn Owls and the breeding Snipe which have forsaken us but has noted an increase in sightings of all three species of Woodpecker in recent years. He believes Sparrowhawks and Magpies are also far more abundant nowadays but the regular Hawfinches seem to have moved on.

Well, a great deal seen already and we haven't taken a step yet. So come on, let's move on up the lane towards the church. At the top of the lane, beyond the handy-heighted Hazel nut bushes, is a stable which is often host in summer to a family of Swallows. So much has been written about this harbinger of spring, what more can be said? But I'll try. Firstly, it is an aviation miracle, travelling thousands of miles each spring and autumn, without air traffic control for guidance and only a few mouthfuls of bugs for fuel. And yet the same Swallow will find the same barn for several years in succession. Just watch a Swallow in its high speed pursuit for mid-air morsels. A dark-topped blur, flicking effortlessly from side to side, its wide open gape slurping up a soup of unsuspecting insects, and its dramatically shaped tail twisting and turning as eagle eyes detect the next tiny target a few inches ahead. Resembling a highly manoeuvrable Batman, this ruby-throated wonder then swoops with great panache through any tiny opening in the barn at forty miles per hour to show off his catch to his family. And then, his duties duly performed, he will ofttimes emerge to sit on the lower stable door right in front of the fortunate observer to entertain with ebullient twitterings. A right show-off perhaps, but many might agree, he's entitled to be.

We are now at Sterlings, the lovely houses straddling the lane towards the church which were built in 1975 on land once owned by the family of that name. Sterlings Lodge remains from an earlier era. The views across the Rise to Cliveden and beyond Lower Mount to Windsor are spectacular on a sunny day. Meanwhile, the small orchard abutting the cemetery is worth a careful scan as many a time one might descry a Great Spotted Woodpecker. Known as French Pie in the past, these entertaining creatures were perfectly designed for their preferred habitat. With their zygodactyl feet (two toes pointing for'ard and two aft), and their exceptionally short and stiff tails, they can scamper about the boughs backwards, forwards, upside down or whatever, seeking out grubs from every nook and cranny using their long bill and even longer tongue. The tongue is up to 20cm long, is sticky and has little hooks at the end; a sort of Velcro shoe-lace really. And if dinner is a little out of reach, well, the pneumatic drill comes into play. Woodpeckers can hammer away without the need for a stock of paracetamol due to a thick, grisly, shock-absorbing pad between the upper mandible and the skull. Not all the hammering noises one hears are nest-boring or food-searching, however. Having not been gifted with a melodious song, the male attracts his mates by decorous drummings on dead branches during spring.

*Great Spotted Woodpecker*

Both mater and pater vociferate at each other with piercing 'chips' and should a clutch of young be overheard clamouring over an unseen breakfast table, echoing from a hollowed bole, it sounds like several mechanical egg-whisks operating simultaneously.

And so on to the cemetery itself, a portal between past and present, with its horizontal resting places and its upward pointing name-plates, as if a final reminder to the Almighty of who resides. A habitat for death all around a building that offers life to those who seek it. Ministering in this enigmatic House, as colleague to Rev Copping, is the Rev Philip Ind, not

*St. John the Baptist Church*

only a notable man of the cloth, but an enthusiastic 'birder' to boot. Philip was born in Chakrata, India where his father Bertie was serving as an Army Schoolmaster with the 17th/19th Bengal Sappers and Miners. Philip himself joined the services, as a Royal Navy cadet at Dartmouth, departing as Sub Lieutenant in 1957 to consider a call to even higher service! Philip met his wife Marie-Thérèse in Durham whilst studying theology. Following ordination in Bury St Edmunds, the couple were married at St John the Baptist Church in the Dean in 1961, returning in 1987 to Stilegate, a family cottage adjacent to Oswalds where Marie-Thérèse's mother, Mrs Antoinette Gunner lives. Stilegate was built on Tugwood Common around 1840 as a home for the gardener of adjacent Beechwood, whilst Oswalds was recorded on the Swinhurst Manor Computation of Tithes Map as far back as 1746. After a twelve-year tour of duty around a number of churches, the Inds returned to Stilegate in 1987.

A keen birdwatcher since his teens, Philip has found the mixed farming and woodland of the Cookhams rich in birdlife with interesting visitors to his garden including the delightful Firecrest. Closely related to the more common Goldcrest, Firecrests have an unmistakable bold white stripe over their large doleful eyes, highlighting further the black and yellow stripe over the crown. Both are members of the warbler family of birds but whilst there is estimated to be half a million Goldcrests throughout the country, there may be only some two hundred singing male Firecrests to listen for in the spring. Fortunately for us, the vast majority of them live in the south east, with almost half breeding in Wendover Woods in Buckinghamshire, so wandering birds in winter are always worth keeping an eye open for. However, most birdwatchers would be really envious of someone having a Firecrest in the garden! Other notable occasions in the vicinity have included the discovery of a family party of Woodcock in Quarry Wood - a mother and three chicks. Woodcock have an uncanny knack of simply freezing perfectly still for minutes on end when they know they have been spotted. They then rely upon their incredibly cryptic plumage to gradually merge them into the surroundings. I have experienced the same thing in Church Wood,

Hedgerley where I peered at a Woodcock for fifteen minutes, slowly wondering if I had seen it at all, only the beady eye convincing me it was still where it had landed. Eventually my arms ached so much I had to let the binoculars down which was the cue for the bird to sidle into the bracken, not to be seen again that day. Regrettably, Woodcock are not likely to be seen in Quarry Wood either these days.

A more regular occurrence is Philip's encounters with Tawny Owls. I have often pondered as to how many remain in the Cookhams, as development and traffic will have taken its toll compared to the quieter times of yesteryear. On the other hand, the remaining tree-line is now more mature which is a more favourable habitat for them. Philip has heard up to four or five males calling from behind the house on one occasion. Whether these were adults or a family of young males competing with dad we cannot know, but there are perhaps more around than we imagine. I well remember walking past the cemetery at dusk one spring and noting a great commotion from within a dense yew tree. It was that time of night when numerous male Blackbirds are signing off with mock alarm calls; the sort of call that often gets us out into the garden assuming a cat is creating havoc, only to find none in sight.

This particular evening, every one of the gardens around the church seemed to have its clucking Blackbird, but the din emanating from the churchyard was much more urgent and involved several birds, including a very agitated Great Spotted Woodpecker. As I drew closer to the tree, the cause of the trouble revealed itself; a fine Tawny Owl swooped out of the tree at low level, gliding silently and effortlessly to a neighbouring garden, pursued triumphantly by a formation of Robins, Blue Tits, Blackbirds and the aforementioned 'pecker. As all this was played out right in front of me, a full grown Roe Deer bounded across the graveyard, leaping over every headstone that deigned to get in its way. My attention thus drawn away from the magnificent owl, I spied it no more that evening, but I have little doubt it was one of the individuals that had given Philip much pleasure over the years.

*Tawny Owls*

Little Owls also make acquaintance with Philip when he is out on Cockmarsh, often two birds alerting each other to his presence. If only those Barn Owls we used to have were there to make up the set, it would be wonderful. A Dipper on Bisham brook provided another exciting moment for him one year, seen later at Little Marlow Gravel Pit. Our local streams generally are too slow to interest this remarkable bird which nonetheless can be quite confiding to the eager discoverer. They are an active bulky Black-bird sized creature, spending most of their time either whizzing up and down the stream on whirring wings just above the water, or standing on a prominent stone in the flow, bobbing up and down like a pantomime policeman. But their most fascinating behaviour is seen when they suddenly leap into the water, facing up-stream and promptly dive underneath to hunt for a snack. They will then emerge, hardly looking damp at all and then repeat the exercise for another morsel. It has been discovered that they simply cannot get enough of Mayfly nymphs and Caddis larvae (there really is no accounting for taste!). However, as the territory map of the Dipper is exactly the opposite of the Firecrest with hardly any at all in the south east, we can only hope for rare glimpses of this cheeky individual. Having said that, I do know of another which was seen on the Thames at Cookham Bridge the following year, so you never know!

Probably one of Philip's 'Most Memorable Birding Moments' was coming across a Cirl Bunting near the railway line along Maidenhead Road in 1961. In those days, both sides of the lane were extensively covered in gorse and it was amongst this covering that he found this extremely rare specimen. Once fairly common in the area, sightings fell dramatically in the post-war years and his liaison with this particular individual may even have been the last for the village. More recently, in 1990, his attention was drawn to an unfamiliar shriek and, on looking up, saw two Cranes flying up the Thames Valley, high over Quarry Woods. Later in the same day, he heard the same shriek again and this time found it to be an escaped Sulphur Crested Cockatiel in a neighbours garden. The earlier flypast of the Cranes had therefore been spotted by pure chance!

Whilst in the vicinity of the church grounds, there is one other summer visitor one might perchance encounter: the Spotted Flycatcher. This fascinating, and perhaps inappropriately named bird is one of the last migrants to arrive after its long journey from its wintering grounds. This is because, as its name implies, it survives essentially on flies and small flying insects, and it needs to be sure these are plentiful upon arrival.

So, it might be late May or even early June before our first glimpses of this active acrobat are ensured. This area of the Dean is one of the few parts of the Cookhams where this species has been spotted. When first we get a close look at this quarry we are entitled to ask "Why *spotted* Flycatcher?" as in fact the bird has no spots at all. Its head, chest and underparts are in fact striated, not spotted as we would see on the Song Thrush, for example. This proves to be yet another example of the peculiar names we have given our birds over the centuries, most likely, I suspect, through the early observers having no optical aids and having to rely on distant visual study only. Hence we get Black-headed Gull, which is white-headed most of the year and only *brown*-headed at best for a short breeding season. We have Goosander, which isn't related to geese at all, a Kentish Plover that you hardly ever see in Kent, a Common Gull that isn't all that common, and a Bearded Tit that isn't a Tit and doesn't have a beard!

Anyway, back to our Striated Flycatcher, or Beam Bird as it was once known, due to its occasional habit of nesting against cross-timbers in roof cavities (though it will equally utilise holes in trees and walls or even nest boxes). This delicate light grey-brown bird has a penchant for formal gardens near large buildings. Oh, it will fare well enough in woodlands and other areas too, but I have encountered most of my Flycatchers in the vicinity of sites such as churchyards, or stately home-style properties such as Odney. I think they simply have ideas above their station about where to set up home, and why not! After all, its habits are quite lofty, one having to search the higher branches to find one. I have never seen one on the ground. With good fortune, however, the Flycatcher's *modus operandi* helps to make its presence easier to detect. Its main method of catching its aerial breakfast is to sit atop a prominent perch, often a dead extension to a healthy tree, watching for an unsuspecting insect to sally by. The bird then darts out in a looping fashion, grasps the prey and immediately returns to its original perch. No sooner has it alighted, than it may well repeat the manoeuvre for 'seconds', and so on until its appetite is sated.

Of course, in the nesting season, it will have many mouths to feed and the adult pair can be observed at great length, each operating from its personal set of perches, harvesting huge beak-fulls of unidentified flying objects to deliver to ever-hungry young. How they manage to catch another without dropping the rest is a mystery to me. Essentially a hole-nesting bird, they can often be seen disappearing into a suitable nook in

*Spotted Flycatcher*

the wall of an old building in which they have elected to raise one, or two families. The male and female are alike, as is the case with many of our bird species. Why were some pairs made identical, and others easily separable? We'll have to ask when we get up there! The male has in indistinct, seedy sort of song, not often detected, but the contact call is more readily picked up, being a high-pitched reedy sort of *seep*. When the young are fledged and they spread themselves out around the various food-catching posts, a whole tree can seem to be filled with this frustrating call, difficult to pinpoint. But with perseverance, this should prove rewarding. In a good summer, and as with many summer visitors, a second clutch may be attempted. Any ensuing inclemency in the weather may spell doom for the second batch of chicks. However, it is recorded that the young from the first brood will assist the parent birds in the feeding of the newer siblings, something I have personally observed only with House Martins.

Now, where shall we go ?

*The Old Farmhouse*

# To the Woods

MUCH WOODLAND HAS BEEN LOST to the area in the last century, but we are fortunate to have a remnant on our doorstep. Quarry Woods was once an established Beech Hanger which looked dramatic from the Bisham side looking up its slopes cloaked in green. Nestling amongst and besides this verdant carpet is Cookham Dean. At that time, there were very few roads, only tracks from one end of the Dean to the other. Water had to be fetched from the spring on Spring Hill or the well in Well Lane. Deadmans pond would still have been in use, little suspecting its imminent filling after the unfortunate death of Dick Hatch whose body within its frozen grip was discovered by my wife's uncle, Jim Skinner.

It was in the lea of this woodland that W H Hudson lodged in a small cottage to seek inspiration for his book a century ago. He noted about a dozen Nightingales in the area, all with a habit of singing during the day, but never at night. Alas, this auditory delight is not available to us today. Nightingales continued to be reported from the area into the thirties but numbers gradually reduced thereafter. The tree coverage would have been different one hundred years ago, and coppicing may well have been practised, before the rich blanket of Beech took over. The storms of 1987 put paid to that, leaving in its wake huge swathes of openness, holes in the bedspread, as it were. But woodland is a remarkable beast and already the sections left open by that hurrying blast have begun to produce a lush under-story that is enriching the flora of the woods and providing greater variety of both plant life and food stocks for birds.

I haven't noticed diminution of any of the species that used to frequent the woods prior to the storm and, if anything, butterfly numbers have increased, and who knows, the open areas may attract Nightingales once more. Perhaps the Woodpeckers have lost many a dead tree in which to nest, but even then, Quarry Wood affords the one opportunity in the Cookhams where all three types of Woodpecker might be found. The most difficult variety to find will always be the Lesser Spotted Woodpecker (or Wood Pie) by virtue of its size, barely equivalent to a sparrow, and the fact that it spends its time feeding on much smaller branches amongst the foliage, whereas its bulkier relative, the Great Spotted 'Pecker is more noticeable on the larger boughs. It is in any case a less numerous bird, there being perhaps only six or seven thousand pairs in the United Kingdom compared to over thirty thousand of the Greater Spotted sort.

Strangely, no woodpeckers of any species are to be found in Ireland. It must be something they said!

But, with luck and perseverance, one may well encounter one of the two or three pairs that probably roam around the Cookhams. Its undulating flight is noteworthy and may be the first clue to having stumbled across one. If it is calling a great deal, it probably *isn't* a Lesser, as they are much less vocal than their larger brother. However, when hammering its springtime nuptials, the Lesser prolongs each drumming far longer than its relative. The black back of the bird, when seen, is notable for its evenly spaced rows of white dots, which earn this cheeky specimen its name. This compares with the large bold corporal stripes down the back of the Great Spotted 'Pecker. The Lesser also possesses a striated chest, not seen on the other species. I was fortunate on one occasion when my eyes alighted upon one of each species with uncommon adjacency, side by side, just 6 inches apart, on the same branch in this woodland. What a wonderful spectacle, and an excellent opportunity to compare them. They seemed quite content, each with the others company, and fed without tetchiness until the smaller member of the party departed, not to be seen again that day.

I suspect the Lesser wanders further than the Greater, which appears contrary to the usual rule of the larger the bird, the larger the territory. If seen closely enough, the male can be separated from the female by his bright red helmet, the hen 'pecker having a white bonnet instead. The juvenile takes after the male's plumage; another peculiarity as most small passerine youngsters resemble the mother bird in first plumage.

Woods can be temperamental and one has to read the resident mood on arrival. One day can be more active than the next, one hour can be dead compared to the previous one. Most have a lunch break where bird activity is concerned. Although fairly quiet most of the time, like all woodland, Quarry Wood is best visited very early in the morning, especially in spring and early summer. The dawn chorus in a British woodland has to be the eighth wonder of the world, yet it is available to us on our doorstep without flights abroad, and what's more, it is free! Aficionados of dawn chori will be on site well before light, as it is well known that it is the song of the birds that requests the onset of daylight. Without its heralding, daytime probably would not bother to arise. In inky darkness, the Robin will most likely act as conductor, with Mr Blackbird in hot pursuit, tuning up the other participants. The strings of the Willow

Warbler and the piccolo 'pinks' of the Chaffinch will follow, only momentarily prefacing any nearby Skylark who in turn will harmonise from on high with the reedy song of a lowly Dunnock. By the time that the hue of dawn is climbing out of bed, the orchestra is in full swing, with finches and warblers, Nuthatches and Tits, crows and pigeons. To us, the conducting might seem somewhat random, though I am persuaded that there is pattern to it somewhere. However, I am content to simply bathe in the experience rather than learn the tune, wondering whether or not they too listen to us!

> *"Do not revile the ruler, even in your thoughts*
> *Or curse the rich man in your secret room,*
> *Because a bird of the air may carry your words,*
> *And a bird on the wing may report what you say."*
> *Eccl 3:20*

With colleagues, and in a slightly more varied woodland environment well west of Cookham, I have counted forty species before daybreak. Perhaps twenty plus is more achievable in the Quarry, but well worth getting up for at least once a year, surely. Besides, once the roadways below around Bisham and Marlow commence their daily hum, it becomes difficult to hear much at all after seven of the a.m. with the fewer trees to block out the din these days.

Quarry Wood was once surrounded by private timberland, restricting the areas for exploration, but Fultness and Inkydown Woods have recently been made available to the woodland wanderer, affording lengthy walks that can now reach across to the Marlow Road to the west and down the slopes to the Marlow Bypass to the north (remembering of course that, having gone down this veritable slalom course, one has to come back up again!). However, it is certainly worth diving down this steep pathway towards Bisham, not only because of the birds one might encounter, but because, at the bottom, lies an old Victorian ice house. Built around 1760, it was the refrigerator of its day, providing ice for the table throughout the year, facilitating ice cream for summer picnics. Constructed of a double layer of hand-made bricks, it has a soakaway drainage system, and is set into the north facing chalk hill, ensuring low temperatures and good drainage. Blocks of ice would have been taken from the Thames and pounded into small fragments to slow down the thawing process. Restored in 1984 by Mr Christopher Wallis, this relic of our recent past can be inspected by means of a key available at the adjacent Smiths Cottage (No 45) or next door at 44.

Other interesting species likely to be encountered in these woods are the Marsh Tit and the Willow Tit. Both of these members of the Titmouse family are brown in general appearance, but with striking black caps. Both are much scarcer than their blue colleagues, especially the Willow. It is only in this last century, since 1897 to be precise, that these two species have been separated, it being previously accepted that all black-headed titmice were Marsh Tits. Again, an inappropriate name applies. The bird is rarely found on marshes and is quite at home in the same habitats as all its tit-peers. To differentiate between the Marsh and the Willow by appearance is nigh on impossible without the clearest of views. The Willow has a slightly larger black bib to catch the gravy on, a dull cap compared to a shiny one for the Marsh, and a light wing panel fashioned by the secondary feathers when folded. Well, I ask you; no wonder most folk used to think them all the same. How on earth are you expected to pick those features out, especially as you usually only see one or the other without anything to compare with!

Well, there is some good news to hear. They sound different! The Marsh Tit, the most likely to be encountered, used to be known as the Coal Head, but I prefer to nick-name it the Sneeze Bird. If you are walking through the woods and hear a bird going 'Tischoo, Tischoo, Tischoo', you know you are near a Marsh Tit. Other squeaks and squeals are similar between the two, but the Willow also has a distinctive 'psiu, psiu, psiu, psiu' invariably repeated four times, which sets it apart from the Marsh. Strangely, neither of these bouncy brownlings venture as far as Scotland, to that nation's loss. But conversely, the third brown titmouse, the Crested Tit, is exclusive to their highland woods, never seen below Hadrian's Wall, as if by edict. And yet this latter species is exceptionally common throughout Europe beyond the Channel. This time, it must be something *we* said!

Back in our neighbouring woodland, many other species queue up to entertain us. Of course, all the other titmice are present in various numbers (I include not the Bearded Tit, which is not a Tit at all but a Reedling). The Blue and the Great impose themselves upon the scene throughout the wooded area, but the Coal Tit seems happier where there are a few conifer trees. This too is a black-capped bird, but with a prominent white stripe from beak to nape over the head. It will spend more time in the higher branches than the other tits but will descend often enough to be recognised. The last member of the clan, and most easily distinguished from the others, is the Long Tailed Tit.

The Long Tailed Tit has had many nick-names in its time, many of them derived from its domed nest with a neck-shaped side entrance. Hence we have had Bottle Tit, Bush Oven, Jug Pot, and even Bum Barrel. The nest will comprise up to two thousand small feathers, a miscellany of lichens and mosses, all bound together with cobwebs. This is design and construction *par excellence*, and yet surprisingly, some still opine that such things have happened purely by accidental origin and the passage of time. Following a general rule that smaller birds lay more eggs than larger ones (though Pheasants seem to be an exception), up to ten or twelve eggs will be laid. When all are hatched, the nest will bulge, writhe and wriggle in harmony with its contents, just as will a small carcass when home to many maggots.

In any event, we are more likely to see only the bird itself, labelled Kitty Longtail by our forebears. What a delightful bird it is too; its almost ridiculously long tail, nearly three inches long, hiding just how tiny it really is. Its colouration is a suffusion of browns, pinks, off-whites and greyish-blacks. Its head is round with the tiniest, shortest bill of nearly all our resident species. And so active! Hardly spending a moment in the same place, it fusses about the shrub level, fortunately about our head height, wheezing and chuntering as it goes.

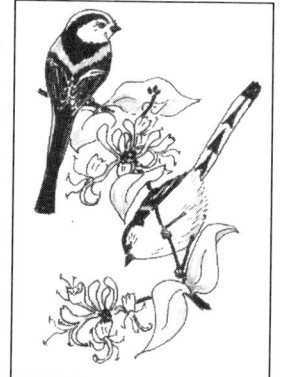

*Long-tailed Tits*

♪"Sorry! Can't stop! Sorry! Can't stop!"♪ it seems to be saying. It also sounds as if it clicks its fingers regularly with a sharp sound, like snapping closed its insignificant bill. This colourful busy-ness is most obvious in autumn and winter as the bird has a proclivity for hunting in feathery packs, commonly fifteen or twenty strong, but I have witnessed over forty together in these woods, presumably four or five families which have joined together to survive the colder months.

There resides, however, an even more striking occupant of these woods, perhaps only to be found in one other place in Cookham. Have you ever walked these woods, or the plantations around the Odney area, and thought you saw a Kingfisher dashing from tree to tree? If so, you will have experienced an encounter with a Nuthatch. This enthralling bird seems to span the arboreal habits of the woodpecker with the musical ability of our flutiest songbirds. In colouration, its steel blue back contrasts with chestnut underparts and a buff-white throat. Its dagger-like beak seems to continue through the head by virtue of a deep black eye stripe. By proportion to its body size, it has enormous feet, with powerful claws. These help it to mimic the behaviour of 'peckers in clambering up trees and branches, and the Nuthatch seems to be alone in the capability of climbing down a bole forwards, despite having a conventional toe arrangement compared to the special design of 'pecker's feet.

As to song, the Nuthatch vies with the Wren for volume and personality. Whilst the latter shouts from the undergrowth, the very canopy is the chosen stage from which the Nuthatch performs. A series of notes reminiscent of the Kestrel kill-call is often first thrown out, followed by a number of penetrating *Tiuee Tiuee Tiuee* calls. Faster, piping *Tchu Tchu Tchu Tchu Tchu* calls may be uttered and strident *pweep pweeps* ensue. What is lacking in variety is more than supplanted by decibels as this ebullient 'tree-fisher' makes his presence known. Noisiest when establishing a breeding territory and later when the young have fledged, the male Nuthatch seems determined not be overlooked by the unsuspecting stroller.

Nest building is another occupation in which Nuthatches set out their speciality stall. Preferring an existing hole to excavating a new one, loose bark and small leaves are used to make the lining, the female doing most of the work. But once inside to commence egg laying, the entrance hole is gradually reduced by packing it with large amounts of mud. This helps to prevent attacks from Starlings and Woodpeckers. When the six to ten eggs are hatched, the adult birds are exceptionally busy finding sufficient food, making hundreds of journeys throughout each day. Soon, the time arrives to tempt the young out of the nest-hole to face their first hesitant flight. This is done again with much ceremony and noise, until all are successfully fledged. Then the adults can return to their diet of nuts. Their technique of jamming a nut in a crack or crevice before bombarding it with their stabbing bill has earned it the nick-name 'Nut Jobber'. Many a tapping sound thought to be a woodpecker will prove to be a Nuthatch beating an unfortunate beechnut into submission in a bark-walled torture chamber.

The nature of the woodland, and its tree species, varies as one wanders along. The sloping Quarry has perhaps the wider variety of trees, and the aforementioned open glades add extra richness. Along the top and heading through Fultness, more deciduous species are encountered, but also significant blue-bell dells, in season. The most western sector has perhaps less under-story growth and attracts more of the higher level residents, especially hoards of Wood Pigeon resting between raids on the nearby farmland. A summer walk from one end to the other, with eyes and ears akimbo, should ensure contact with most of our common warblers, the six species of Titmouse referred to, plus Treecreepers (of which more later), Jackdaws, Song Thrushes, Kestrel, perhaps Sparrowhawk and others besides.

Another good time to experience the special atmosphere of these woods is early on New Years Day, especially if it has snowed or there is a good coating of frost about. With every branch glistening, and every sound reverberating over and over again, we are given a completely different sensation. A Wren bursts out from her lair at our approach, exploding into chiding song, warning every other arboreal creature of our presence. An inquisitive Robin alights on a nearby branch, tipping a spoonful of snow onto the branch below, his plumage seeming even more brilliant than normal in the eerie bright air. Droplets of crystal fall from the canopy, dislodged by a watery sun and shadows of Crows and Pigeons chase each other along the woodland pathways. Flocks of finches, possibly including Brambling, hurl ghostly white leaves over their shoulders in search of a late breakfast and Great Spotted 'Peckers *Tchat* from on high. Blackbirds and Song Thrushes thrust about in darkened larders and, with good fortune, a group of Goldcrests might descend to inspect you at close quarters, doffing their bright crowns in salute. With less foliage to obstruct your view, Quarry Wood in winter is most certainly worth a visit, but take your wellies!

Woodland in winter also speaks of a contrast—of beauty and of survival. Severe cold snaps, lasting a number of days, will stretch the survivability of small birds to the limit. With such a thin covering of flesh to cover their vital organs, small birds need to take on almost their own weight in food each day to generate enough energy to keep warm at night. With frozen ground, and a covering of snow, this becomes impossible. It was estimated that the terrible winter of 1967 reaped over sixty percent of the nation's Wrens, and untold millions of other species. We should marvel that such tiny creatures as the Wren can indeed make it through these stringent times to remain in territory to entertain us, even if she does try to let on when we turn up! Her whistles and churrs echo about, urging our immediate departure.

A peculiar thing I've noticed about alarm calls however, is that individual species seem to totally ignore the alarm calls of others. Wrens alert Wrens, Blackbirds dial 999 for other Blackbirds and so forth, but rarely seem to trigger each other into action. I've watched Mistle Thrushes fighting off Jays with horrendous noise, all else around totally unconcerned. I've seen a Sparrowhawk take a Great Tit and consume it in a bush, surrounded by other indignant Great Tits, but totally ignored by a singing Yellowhammer. I could recount many other such occurrences. Somewhat odd, but at least it means the Wren's early warning system will not prevent you seeing other birds.

Having mentioned Jays, it is interesting to compare the success of this striking bird with that of its close relative the Magpie. In his accounts of birding in Quarry Wood a century ago, Hudson recalls that, despite much hope and many hours prospecting, he never found a Magpie in the area. He did make contact with one or two Jays however, and even today one is relatively fortunate to encounter this magnificent creature. A member of the crow family, it is by far the most striking in plumage, with pinky-brown underparts and back, an iridescent blue patch on black

*Magpie*

and white wings, a streaked crew-cut on the crown, sporting a black moustache and the most brilliant white rump whilst in departure mode. Per its peers, it is a boisterous and bullying bird and its head looks quite fearsome close to. Its harsh call adds to its rapacious reputation and most assuredly, the territory around Quarry Wood suits it perfectly. So why has it not multiplied in the intervening one hundred years?

Of the Magpie by contrast, modern day villagers would be surprised at its erstwhile scarcity. Nowadays, it is a common sight, and sound, in our gardens, the park, the surrounding fields and hedgerows. There may perhaps be as many as one hundred to be seen around the Cookhams. In considering the reasons for this entirely different prosperity, several thoughts come to mind. Firstly, by nature the Magpie is a farmland bird, preferring to nest some eight to ten feet up in dense Hawthorn hedges.

Regrettably, the larger proportion of our nation's hedges have been systematically removed in the last half century by virtue of 'improved' farming techniques. In addition, they were often shot off farmland being regarded as a pest, especially if Pheasants or Grouse were being raised for commercial purposes as Magpies have a penchant for fresh eggs. One might assume that this would have spelt the end of the Magpie but, over the same period of years the gardens of houses erected in the same era have become mature with many hedges, trees and bushes which constitute suitable alternative nesting sites. Furthermore, the owners of these new 'mini-farms' have relinquished the habit of using the bird for target practice and are even so good as to put food out for them (so far as the Magpie is concerned, anyway). Finally, compared to the Jay, Magpies appear more confiding insofar as proximity to man is concerned.

Added together, these factors have resulted in the Pie being a common sight in our midst and should we take the time to withhold a curse and look closely at the bird, we might be surprised how attractive it is to the eye. Too easily dismissed as a 'black and white job', the Magpie is in fact constructed of many hues of blue and sheens of green, mostly iridescent and thus affording different effects in varying light conditions. In wintertime, groups of them gather together for a chin-wag, cackling excitedly as more and more join the fray. I have counted as many as 49 together in one of these open-air seminars but have failed thus far in my life-time to discern their topic of discussion or motive for this operandi. Perhaps just where the next meal will come from?

> *Look at the birds of the air;*
> *They do not sow or reap*
> *Or store away in barns,*
> *And yet your heavenly Father feeds them.*
> *Are you not much more valuable then they?*
> *Matthew 6:26*

Anyway, time to explore some new territory, I think. How about a more open prospect?

# WHERE SAXONS LAY

TRAPPED IN THE HAM OF THE THAMES to the north of the village is an open expanse known as Cockmarsh, complete with its burial mounds and ancient history. It would once have been a relatively remote and undisturbed quarter of our heavenly setting, but significantly ravaged by no lesser person than Isambard Kingdom Brunel who, as Great Western Railway's Chief Engineer, responded to demands for a linking of the Wycombe Railway to the GWR station in Maidenhead. With construction commencing in 1852 at a cost of some £60,000, a wide gauge track was laid down upon a wooden river crossing. A high bank was built on the marsh to overcome the flooding problem and Winter Hill was severed by a deep cutting which now separates some of the holes on the modern golf course. Hardly had life restored to normal for the Marsh wildlife than Isambard was back to reconstruct the line as standard gauge.

Perhaps a little drier these days than heretofore, the marsh tempts us with the prospect of some different species of birds. Also, it embraces a number of interesting properties along the river bank, seemingly cut off from the rest of the world. In fact for some, without a significant fee to adjacent landowners, they would be! One of these is in fact an inn, called The Bounty. Not that it was always known by that name; the site was originally The Quarry Hotel, a 30-bed Victorian place of harbourage built in the 1880's. In it's heyday, many

*The Quarry Hotel*  *Cockmarsh 'Aerodrome'*

a famous visitor came to stay and, with access restricted as it still is today, a private airstrip was the main means of arrival. Miles Magisters, Puss Moths and the like would ply the invisible highways to numerous remote aerodromes carrying the revellers to an escapist weekend on the banks of the great river Thames, overlooked by the sweeping slopes of

Winter Hill. There are even rumours that Edward the king, and Mrs Simpson availed themselves of the hospitality of this place. It was during this era that the good people of Cookham raised some money for the protection of Cockmarsh and allotted it to the National Trust for safe preservation in 1934. Regrettably, the Quarry Hotel itself perished in flames in 1938, with the sad loss of two members of staff.

Eventually, the present building was erected, utilising part of the remaining rear wall and the dance floor, which survived the ravages of the flames. Initially it took the form of tea rooms, and was owned by an opera singer. Subsequently, and in the guise of The Moorings Inn, it came under the ownership of none other than Captain Hook! This was the name given to Peter Lane who had suffered the misfortune of losing both hands in an accident. He could pull a pint with his hook with great deftness but, after 14 years, Peter moved to Ross on Wye, opening the opportunity for the present owners, David and Sue Wright, to take over in 1987. The pub took its new name, The Bounty, from the show *Mutiny* which starred David Essex at the time. Sue was an ardent Essex fan so the name became obvious and also gave rise to its unique bar. Apart from the original footbridge, and the more recent footway, glued onto the side of the railway bridge, a regular ferry service across the Thames was the only way of getting from Bucks into Berks and to stop off for a pint. The Thames Conservancy closed the local ferry from Spade Oak in the late '50's and even the private service from the Townsend Yard ceased at the same time. The Bounty would have been a popular reason for an evening crossing and doubtless many a shivoo will have been held there. Nowadays, passing trade is still rife and a pleasant discovery for the long-distant Thames Rambler on a hot summers day, or a wet wintry one! Deliveries continue to be by boat from the chandlers yard on the Bucks bank.

David likes to get out early in the morning and walk in the attractive countryside that envelopes The Bounty. Having been brought up on incredible numbers of waders that used to visit the Perry Oaks sewage farm near Colnbrook from where he hails, David has found Cookham's bird life somewhat more rural in nature. He has seen Kestrel numbers increase in recent years and Kingfisher numbers fluctuate greatly, from just one or two up to around nine in the best years. One of David's 'Memorable Birding Moments' was the arrival of a Little Egret which occupied a stretch of bankside just a few yards beyond the pub for a time in 1995.

One common scene for much of the year is varying number of Lapwing on the marsh. Each year, a small number attempt to breed, but constant disturbance from walkers, and trampling bovines results in poor success rates. From autumn through to early spring, a 'desert' of as many as one thousand of these magnificent waders spread out over the marsh. A more striking creature is difficult to find. The Eurasian member of a family of twenty five different types of Lapwing, we are most fortunate to possess one of the most colourful. The bird's noble head, suffused with buff and black, is crowned with regal black plumes of notable length. Caped with iridescent greens above (from which it earns the alternative name Green Plover), the underparts are a snowy white. A deep black chain of office is sported high upon the chest, and when bowing to feed, a striking orange patch beneath the tail is displayed. Strutting with royal gait, a field of these gorgeous birds are reminiscent of a Singer sewing machine test workshop, with heads bobbing up and down as each clod is inspected for grubs.

But it is in the air that this prince of birds establishes his realm. Even in general flight, the peculiarly-shaped wing draws our attention. The only British bird with wing tips broader than wing roots, the flying action resembles two broad canoe paddles in unison, enhanced by the contrasting views of dark green above and brilliant white below. Disporting this top-hat and tails plumage, a skein in formation looks like a mass performance of 'We're a Couple of Swells'.

---

## APRIL

Winter frowns, is letting go
Newness forms in Heavens beau
Sun and ice contest God's space
What sparkling splendour surrounds this place.

> Dashing Hawks in aerial ballet
> Herons gliding through the valley
> Linnets, Larks and Cuckoo too,
> Serenading just for you.

Huge numbers can be seen wheeling about the sky when disturbed, invariably coming to rest right where they first departed. This particular flock wanders between this location and the open field near Bisham, whilst a similar number occupy the fields between Summerleaze Gravel Pit and Lower Mount. If you see a large number in the air, you are likely to note smaller birds amongst them. These are not young Plovers as often supposed but invariably Starlings who seem happy to fly amongst these aerial champions, perhaps to learn a trick or two. A more likely reason could be protection, as I am not sure I have ever heard of a Sparrowhawk attacking adult Lapwings, maybe because of their remarkable agility.

However, whilst the formation displays are dramatic enough, it is when an individual decides to show off that the sparks fly. Prompted by the pangs of springtime, the male bird will fling himself seemingly uncontrollably about the sky, flicking from airway to airway in flamboyant fashion. Dashing headlong towards the ground, he will suddenly pull upwards only to barrel-roll into yet another death-defying manoeuvre. Twenty-point hesitation rolls, inside loops, outside loops, stall turns, wing-overs - this feathered Pitts Special possesses the full repertoire. Not that the male alone manifests these skills. A nosy Crow at fledgling time will evince a simultaneous barrage of exaggerated swoops from both cock and hen plovers. And during all of this display, its evocative *peeewit peeewit* calls are uttered, just to remind of yet another name for this bird. Other names from a bygone age include Flop Jack and Corn Willen.

*Lapwings*

Only a few remain in summer to attempt breeding. Most of our British Lapwings move west to raise their young, but even in their preferred breeding grounds, Peewits suffer the same problems of modern farming practice and numbers continue to decline year by year. Nevertheless, there are estimated to be some two hundred thousand pairs remaining in Britain, so we should be blessed with their presence for a while yet.

If in fact the odd pair do manage to raise young on Cockmarsh, the juveniles are fun to see. Did you ever see the film 'Star Wars' with those huge two-legged metal monsters walking about. Well, imagine one of those covered in flecked down and you have a baby Peewit. All legs, and able to scamper about very soon after hatching; necessary when you have your own four-legged monsters trampling about all around you chewing the cud. Their first reaction when being alarmed by ever-watchful parents is to freeze and make themselves as small as possible, their cryptic feathering keeping them hidden. However, they thrive much better if not disturbed at all so please, please, please, don't go walking across the marsh in spring and summer. If you are out for a stroll and wish to get to the river from Winter Hill, please walk round the outside or follow the footpath through the field to the west.

Once at the river, there are more species to keep an eye open for (or preferably, both). One of these will be the Great Crested Grebe, a truly spectacular bird in summer attire. If prizes were to be awarded for good looks, this would be one of the species that possessed a handsome trophy cabinet. Its dark, tufted crown contrasts with a white face and a pink, stabbing bill. The long neck is white at the front and black down the back, and hanging down from the cheeks of the bird is a mantilla of chestnut and black plumes down the neck. The back is dark grey/brown and the underparts are a contrasting buff and rust. On the water it is an exceedingly elegant bird, separating the surface effortlessly when diving for small fish, resulting in it's ancient name of 'Douker' (or, for the strangest of reasons, 'Tommy Allan' if you happen to live on Lindisfarne!). Usually only under the water for 15 seconds or so, it soon emerges with its latest catch. The Grebe's courting ritual is also picturesque, the pair approaching each other with much accompanying music, then rising up together from the water on thrashing webbed feet, chest-to-chest, their heads shaking wildly from side-to-side, bills touching and often exchanging a morsel of food as part of the sequence.

This aquatic Torville and Dean ballet concluded, attention is given to the nest and raising of progeny. These little balls of down too are very cute. If you have ever tried one of those competitions in a newspaper or magazine, where a black and white maze is presented, and you have to find your way from one end to the other, you will appreciate the plumage of Great Crested Grebe nippers. The Maker simply wrapped each in one of these competition layouts and put a stubby little bill on the front. I have yet to find time to compare individual young to see whether or not they wear the same competition, but perhaps one day I will. Particularly engaging is the adult's habit of carrying the young on its back, following the other parent bird who will be diving for small fish, often all three or four being transported as if by royal carriage from one restaurant to another. Juveniles retain the stripy head patterns even when fully grown, until their following breeding term next year.

Another bird likely to be encountered near the river, in summer at least, is the Common Tern. Now whilst the Grebe is a master of the water, the Common Tern can boast alacrity above and below the surface. Most elegant in the air, it wanders along the Thames from the ternery at nearby Little Marlow Gravel Pit. Perhaps the fish in the river have a different flavour from those in the pit, just as my family have found when we have held fish-and-chip tasting evenings with samples from all the chippies in the district. For whatever reason however, Common Terns can be seen feeding along the river, despite ample provisioning at the Pit. A flashing white and grey bird, its tight-fitting black cap and brilliant red bill are quickly discerned. Less obvious will be the black tip to the bill which separates this species from the Arctic Tern which often traverses the county in small numbers in Spring. Well trained in table manners, the Tern's feeding habits are immaculate. A dancing flight above the surface, a dip or two lower to check a sighting then a half wing-over before an extravagant vertical dive into the water, its wings folding Tornado-style an instant before penetrating the glassy surface of the water. It then emerges with some unsuspecting sprat wriggling in its bill and, with much hoarse self-applause, bounds off to the nest to present the spoils of his sortie.

A common link with these two under-water feeders has been the gradual change of habitat in the county in recent decades. It seems hard to credit that the Great Crested Grebe had all but become extinct in this country just over 100 years ago. Its gorgeous plumes favoured for the millinery trade, they had been harvested in extraordinary numbers for some time when, around 1860, two ladies in the trade recognised the danger facing the bird (and therefore their chosen profession!). Together, they began gathering support for a campaign to protect the species and, after a few years of increasing momentum, this grass-roots movement became something we are very

*Great Crested Grebe*

familiar with today - the Royal Society for the Protection of Birds. The Grebe became the official symbol of the RSPB as, for many decades, they worked to restore the numbers of this magnificent bird. One significant element in the success story of the Grebe has been the emergence of many gravel pits to serve the frenetic building and road-laying industries. Few counties have had more such sites developed than Berkshire, and at each one, numbers of Grebe have quickly moved in to exploit this man-made life-saver. It is now quite possible to see several hundred Great Crested Grebes together on over-wintering waters.

This same factor has greatly increased the number of Common Terns in our vicinity. Previously rarely encountered inland apart from occasional passage movements, this delightful fairy of the air can nowadays be encountered on many of our county waters, regularly raising young on islands or gravel-filled rafts provided especially for this purpose. Assuming increasing numbers of Mink do not exact too great a toll on the numbers of young, the Terns will continue to grace the skies around Cookham's river for many years to come.

A regular walker of the marsh is my friend and next-door neighbour Bill Beglow. Bill often walks his two Collies there, along with his wife Jackie. He's one of the few you might spot with bins on, cocked and ready to go (the bins, not the Collies!). Jackie was a Maidonian, as were her parents, the Hoggs, and she recalls the high class butchers shop in Ellington Road run by Mr John Field, of whom more later. Bill has been a bird watcher for over twenty years and moved to Cookham in 1978. He became a founder member of the East Berkshire RSPB Group after listening to a talk by a well-known Maidenhead birdwatcher, Tony Hawkins, a local bobby. (Strange how many local birders are policemen. The notable bird artist Gordon Langsbury was the constable for Hurley Village and Colin Humphrey, a local birder, is a copper too). Bill went on to form a local Young Ornithologists Group with his colleague Dave Fuller. The success of this training venture was measured in part by the fact that a local Cookham lad, Andrew Goldsmith, went on to become an RSPB Warden.

Amongst Bill's most 'Memorable Birding Moments' in the village was finding his first Lesser Spotted Woodpecker in Southwood Road, where the bird had stoically head-butted a patio door. Fortunately, it recovered, giving Bill a 'tick'. (A 'tick' is a new species added to the observers list of birds seen, and dead ones don't count!). Yet another coincidence, as my first sighting of this species was also in the village, in Long Lane. Bill also recalls being summoned to another garden in Southwood Road to see a 'Snipe' that had been there for a while. He was amazed to find in fact that a Woodcock had taken the garden over for feeding, during a harsh spell of weather. Jackie would not regard herself as a 'serious' birdwatcher but she too has had her ornithological moments in the area, most notable for her being the Little Egret on Cockmarsh in 1995. This is an extremely rare bird inland in this country. "Are Herons sometimes small and white?" she asked me naively one evening. "Not normally" said I, beginning to grit my teeth, aware of an Egret rumoured in the area that we birders had been trying to locate all week. "Oh, I saw one a few days ago on the marsh, so I guess it must have been an Egret". "Did Bill check it out?" I asked. "Oh, I haven't thought to mention it to him" she responded. I was glad not to be in earshot when she eventually got round to mentioning it. However, the bird stayed local for a few more days and Bill and Jackie saw it together on one of their regular outings on the marsh, being fortunate to spot a Wheatear the same day. Small wonder that this area is one of Bill's favourite walks.

A feature of the marsh is its passage birds, those who pop in and out each spring and autumn, rarely staying for more than a day or so. Regular amongst these in April and May will be the Yellow Wagtail. Spectacular in bright buttery plumage, small groups may be found searching for insects to fuel up for their onward flight to the Midlands and beyond. They used to be more common in Berkshire but in recent years have passed through our picturesque plains in almost pitifully small numbers. I well remember counting over 100 between Cockmarsh and the sewage plant some years ago, but can go a whole season without seeing one in the eastern half of the county at all nowadays. The only other bird you are likely to mistake them for are their brethren, the Grey Wagtails. Greys are resident and breed along the Thames and at the aforementioned sewage farm. As their name implies, they have a notable grey back and should be distinguishable from our Yellow traveller at a reasonable distance.

If the Yellow Wagtail is seen more often passing through in spring, the afore-mentioned Wheatear is perhaps more likely to be found here in the autumn, on its return trip. Essentially a summer visitor to much of Europe and Scandinavia, the majority of the British breeding population of some fifty thousand pairs whistle straight through to Wales, Scotland and the north of England. This was not always the case but open areas and downland slopes in the south have been ploughed in recent decades, destroying this chunky bird's favourite habitat. What a striking bird! Bold and upright, moving swiftly over short-grassed fields on long sturdy legs, one minute atop a hump to spy out the land, the next scurrying along a rut to re-appear some yards away. The female is resplendent in her buffs and creamy browns, mixed together like a caramel dessert, the tail edged in black as an exquisite contrast. The male resembles the Lone Ranger with a smoky-grey cap and cape, accentuated by his black mask. Just when you think you have taken in this breathtaking design, it suddenly flits off to another patch revealing a brilliant white patch on the rump, conveniently provided so that you don't lose the bird when it moves. Against the green background of Cockmarsh, it would be hard to hide, but in its natural breeding areas of rabbit-burrowed downland and rocky screes at higher altitude, these contrasting colours meld with the natural greys and browns.

I have to admit to having a soft spot for the Wheatear as it was this species that got me interested in bird watching. As a seven or eight-year old on my father's allotment one day, I saw a bird that clearly wasn't the usual Sparrow or Starling that frequented his cabbage patch. It stayed on the pathway, seemed ever alert and upright and neither my father or his neighbouring plot-holders knew what it was. Not until some five years had passed and I chanced to peep into an Observers Book of Birds in a shop did I find out that it was indeed a Wheatear. The following Christmas, I got this fabled tome in my stocking. I was hooked! And the 'Stone Chack' has remained one of my favourites ever since.

Before a recent spate of mild winters and dry summers, Cockmarsh, and its margins at the foot of Winter Hill, were much wetter and more inaccessible. One Mr Giles recorded Snipe nesting here in 1934, and the Jack Snipe he flushed in January 1936 was probably at the same location. These conditions would regularly tempt another specialist wetland bird to visit, and often breed, in this area. It was the Redshank, so named because of its long, bright red legs. I have seen this boisterous and noisy wader raise its young at the very edge of the boggiest portion of Cockmarsh it could find. Regrettably, this happened to be within a few feet of one of the busier footpaths towards Winter Hill and the constant disturbance eventually proved too much for the pair who, in due course, forsook this site for a quieter life elsewhere. We should mourn the loss, as breeding sites for wader species in the county are becoming fewer and fewer.

Ill-advised county planning officers and gravel pit company managers have restored far too many of the county's wealth of wetlands "to the benefit of the whole community". This translates into steep-sided holes in the ground filled with water, a doggie-walking path provided all round the edge, about one foot away from the water, fishing points approximately every ten feet, sailing and water skiing on the surface, an overgrown island in the middle for "nesting birds" and all the under-water weeds (which might actually attract the odd duck or two) dragged out regularly in case anglers got their tackle stuck in it! Then a sign is erected saying "Country Park and Wildlife Conservation Area". The only birds likely to thrive on such a site are Mallards, Canada Geese and Coots, but let's face it, if you put a saucer of water on your back patio, you'd get Coots nesting on it in a month! Oh for a small number of restored gravel pits with no fishing or sailing, no paths around the water's edge. Reed beds and natural foliage encouraged and gently sloping banks for waders to own. No water sports to disturb over-wintering ducks and gulls, plenty of bottom vegetation for diving species and sheltered approaches to hides from within which we can enjoy the scenes before us without intruding. There are probably more gravel pits per square inch in Berkshire than most other counties in England and yet the amount of really valuable conservation benefit that has resulted is pitifully small. Let us hope the remainder will be restored may be re-created more sensitively.

Hopefully, however, Cockmarsh will continue to produce some of the more unusual visiting species such as the Little Egret mentioned above. If more interest is taken by regular walkers of this splendid piece of landscape, our understanding of the importance of this habitat for passage birds will increase. So please make a note of what you see and let the local bird recorders know. It could be that there is more avian activity there than we realize.

Anyway, its time for a change of scenery.

*Little Egret with Canada Goose on Cockmarsh*

# A STROLL DOWN THE STRAND

SOME YEARS AGO, THE LOCAL COUNCIL established a rambling route from the Thames at Cockmarsh north to Maidenhead, know as the Greenway. Parts of this route abuts Strand Water, a narrow but important stream running from Cookham Moor to North Town Moor in the town, bisecting farmland en route and attracting some interesting birds. A picturesque starting place for an exploration of this part of Cookham would be Strand Lane and its paddocks. Footpaths at the bottom invite a decision whether to go left or right. Either will do, leaving time to explore the other direction next time. More than once I have allowed myself an hour or two for a circular walk, only to find I never got further than the lane itself. Deceptively 'ordinary', one needs to take time along this leafy section to absorb the true atmosphere available. The ambience of the lane requires ferreting out, as if it is too shy to shout its hidden treasures from the roof-tops. The lane itself, for much of its length, is high-hedged with occasional Oaks. Scurry along it and I guarantee you might see nothing, but stop every now and then and you will find this hedge full of Robins, Hedge Sparrows (which are not Sparrows at all, but more of this later), Wrens, Blue Tits, Great Tits, Long-tailed Tits, Blackbirds, Song Thrushes, Greenfinches, Chaffinches and Goldcrests.

The small field adjacent, with its own sparse Oaks, and often hosting a small number of cattle, will hold numerous Collared Doves, Woodpigeons, Yellowhammers, Linnets, occasional Little Owls and for the lucky observer, a Lesser Spotted Woodpecker. The small gravel pit and its shrubbery on the other side houses nesting Moorhens and Coots, Blackcaps, Whitethroats and Willow Warblers in summer, Grey and Red-legged Partridges around its edges, often with Pheasants nearby, Green Woodpeckers and Mistle Thrushes. Kingfishers pay not infrequent visits, even breeding here one year. I have also seen Spotted Flycatchers feeding young here.

*Pheasant*

Pressing on to the paddocks at the end of the lane, the vista opens up slightly affording views over the farmland toward Maidenhead and Summerleaze Gravel Pit. But before looking too far away, a careful scan of the stable areas and piles of straw may prove worthwhile. Many a dalliance with a party of Chaffinches in winter has been rewarded with small numbers of Bramblings in the mix. Shuffling around the floor, in active and easily-disturbed gangs, these thick-billed finches hunt for seeds and small insects. Male, female and juvenile Chaffinches provide a fair range of plumage and colouration, but a Brambling will stand out quite readily, especially if it is a male. Darker on top and more orange-buffish below, the Brambling's most striking signature is its white rump, more obvious in flight. If the group should fly away, don't immediately leave in disgust; they often return almost immediately. You and I are not allowed to know what it is that keeps putting a group of feeding finches up into the trees every few moments, only to return promptly. Imaginary scarecrows? Snails sneezing? Who knows! It is rarely obvious and must waste a lot of precious winter energy, but they do not seem to mind their skittery nature, so why should we? At least it helps us spot those white rumps!

The fence-lines around the paddocks are always worth checking for Jays, Magpies and occasional Little Owls. The larger trees here also host Greater Spotted and Green Woodpeckers and Moorhen pick up take-away meals, scampering off to the nearby stream with them. I have seen as many as 48 of these colourful 'brook squealers' in one of these paddocks. A closer look at a Moorhen reveals its spectacular paintwork. A red and yellow bill contrasts dramatically with a velvety black head and chest. Its browny-black back in turn sets

*Moorhens*

off a purplish side panel, edged in white. Its stubby tail, when raised, reveals a miniature rounded peacock-like arrangement in striking white, it often being bobbed in annoyance at us or in pleasure at a passing dolly-hen. Its ridiculously long legs and partly webbed feet are a sulphury green-yellow. That's what I call design craftsmanship. A certain proximity is permitted, but one step nearer and the whole lot will hoist up their skirts and rush headlong into the reeds or waterside foliage, where they will sit tight until you have gone, even if you throw a grenade in. The Moorhen holds another surprise for us by often clambering up to a high perch in an overhanging tree.

Another species often overlooked is the previously referred to Collared Dove. There are few colonisation success stories as that which applies to this particular bird. As we survey the gallery of doves in the dead trees along the lane, perhaps encountering thirty or forty birds at one time, it seems hard to comprehend that the bird first bred on these great isles as recently as 1955. A bird originating from Australasia, it much favours farm-yard gleanings and proximity to humankind, both of which it found in abundance once over our shores. Having quickly stormed this ecological niche, it went on to populate every county in the UK. Unlike the woodpeckers, it swiftly moved on to conquer Ireland too. By 1964 a census determined a probable population of three thousand pairs. By 1972, this was more like twenty thousand pairs and by now there are some two hundred thousand breeding territories in our nation.

To an extent, this is a great irony. The surpluses of our farming have attracted a new species in extraordinary numbers, but the practices leading to these surpluses are gradually destroying the breeding habitats of many of our traditional British birds. However, this newcomer is quite a striking specimen, its uniform ashy-brown back and buff underparts set against its deep red eye with its black centre, black beak and wing-tips. It possesses a dark brown neck-tie, sometimes edged in white, and unfastened at the front, but let's not be too picky about his dress sense. With much nasal whirring, it flaps hesitatingly from bough to bough, deceleration upon final approach achieved with a broad black and white tail fanned out as a spoiler. It walks along branches, or roof-tops, issuing incessant *coo-coo, coo-coo* notes from dawn to dusk, winning it neither musical awards nor plaudits from anyone beneath trying to sleep!

## MAY

    A chorus of dawn, and hope is re-born
    Eggshells and spawn, clambering corn.
    Life in the root, borne by each shoot
    Joy is the fruit, of summer's new suit.

        Alarmed, dabchicks whinney from sparkling waters
        Reed Buntings warning their sons and their daughters
        For Foxes and Magpies, Kestrels and Stoats
        Are all busy searching for freshly-fledged throats!

Its nest is no more than a pathetic flat platform of loosely-bound twigs and its plump, pimply offspring are initially nourished on milk produced by the parents from their own digested foodstuffs. Whether numbers will now even off or go on to exceed pest proportions is not known, but personally I regret missing the era of Corncrakes, Shrikes and Cirl Buntings in the Cookhams compared to our more pigeonised surroundings.

But worry not! There are still many high-born and dandy occupants of our very own Strand yet to be encountered. Having set off in a northerly direction along the footpath, our next quarry may be heard before being seen. Whilst walking between the paddock fences towards the stile, a song may well beckon from the fields beyond, usually uttered from the top of a hedge or overhead wires. Repetitive and weedy, the words of the ditty are clear; ♪ *"a little bit of bread and no cheeeeze"*.♪ Quick! Get those binoculars I recommended into action. No, further left. That's it, now focus. Got it? What can you see? If you are looking at the same one as me, you should see a bird resembling a brown-backed Canary. Resplendent in a golden-yellow streaked head and chest, with a striking rump of orange-brown, the male Yellowhammer is always an enjoyable find. Of ancient fields and mystical times, many other names have been affixed to this sulphur spectacle; Yeldrock, Yellow Yite, Yellow Yowley, Golden Gladdie and Goldspink to recall some of these.

With great tenaciousness, its plaintive request will be sung over and over again, usually from one of three or four favoured song-posts. Then, as if to consider a different menu, he will spend an hour or two uttering *'think! think! think!* calls. If disturbed, the bird will often lead you along a hedge-row, moving on a few yards each time you get a little too close, displaying its white-edged tail as it flits from station to station. Male and female are usually seen together except during hatching time. The hen bird is far less colourful, a neccssity considering the time spent on the ground-level nest during which camouflage is essential. It's good to be less obvious sometimes. I once saw a male of this species hit fair and square by a full-speed Sparrowhawk in mid air. The Gladdie was knocked about 30 feet and landed upside-down. It righted itself and flew off before the hawk could organise a second run, leaving behind a trail of yellow and white feathers which I proceeded to count. Small passerines have some 1500 to 2000 feathers, (compared to around 20,000 on the magnificent Mute Swan). No less than 346 had been surgically removed in an instant, and yet the bird flew as if unimpeded in any way. Amazing what adrenaline can do, isn't it!

In a good season, a pair may raise three broods. Despite this, the numbers of these Yellow Buntings are falling gradually in our area. In winter-time, Yellowhammers tend to group together, quite sizeable flocks occurring in harsh weather. It is more usual, however to find perhaps twenty or thirty in this area of Cookham, foraging in the pastures with Finches and Sparrows. A bird that is as much at home on heaths, conifer plantations and farmland, it has experienced changing fortunes in the development progress in the south and the modernisation of farming techniques. But whilst this stunning addition to our local avifauna can still be found, let us be thankful.

The fields between the paddocks and The Moor , and over towards Moor Hall, present opportunity to see more Lapwings, winter thrushes, Skylarks and Meadow Pipits, but halfway along, a footpath to the right leads to a return route along the opposite bank of the stream, Strand Water. Slower and wider at this point, the rill and its marginal vegetation is host to some other interesting characters. On the water, the mandatory Moorhen will often be joined by nesting Coot or loafing Mallards and Tufted Ducks.

The Tufted Duck is more at home on open waters such as gravel pits and reservoirs, but can be inspected at closer quarters on this stretch of glistening highway. The male resembles a floating Lapwing, with equally long head-dress plumes. The female is brown and somewhat nondescript. However, whilst their dress may not match the males, the speed with which they depart if you dally too long in proximity certainly does.

*Tufted Duck Family*

A pair of Mute Swans raise a family here most years and once in a while, a fine Heron pops in for a spot of angling. Now there's a specialist if ever there was one. Herons have been associated with the Cookhams for centuries, the network of brooks and tributaries from the Thames providing a rich habitat for them. There has been a Heronry in the Taplow and Cliveden area for many years and birds will casually soar across from their tree-top nests to hunt around the riparian surroundings of the village.

In flight, Jack Herne appears belaboured, his huge wings flapping at only about one beat per second, his neck doubled back over his shoulders and his incredibly long legs trailing behind. Seen closely in the air, the rear toes can be seen carried upright, like an aircraft tail fin, though I have seen many that do not actually do this. Like some prehensile creature, he circles over a likely feeding area, totally oblivious to the unwelcome attention of many a Crow or Rook who object to his presence, and then alights in ungainly fashion to commence the hunt. Herons will take frogs, toads, newts and other bankside creatures as well as fish and eels. When his task is to support Moll Herne whilst she is on the nest, he will help himself to one or two morsels and take the rest back to her. Close up, the proportions of the Heron are peculiar. Whilst once hunting for a Water Rail along Strand Water, I approached a hump on hands and knees in a thick covering of frost, determined for a change to see my quarry before he saw me. Slowly lifting my head above the hump, I came face to beak with a Heron, less than three feet separating us. I think his eyes were even bigger than mine. As Jack departed in a flurry of wings, legs and neck, I had just a few seconds to realise just how small the body is on this otherwise pentamerous creation; about Mallard size seems right. (By way of a departure, I might say that the Water Rail seems not a bird to be found regularly in our area. This one appears to have over-wintered just this once and has not been encountered there again since though I did espie one a few hundred yards downstream a few years later).

*Heron*

Reverting to the Heron, nor is it only at the waters edge that we will find this attractive grey, black and white bird, with its surplice of white plumes. Quite often one or more can be seen standing in the middle of fields, like sentinels to the crops. Looking rather dejected, they resemble unwanted husbands dismissed from the nest whilst the hoovering is being done, or a preacher between sermons. They don't seem to feed, or move about; just stand and sulk, for hours if undisturbed, and then if they are, its a loping, despondent flight over to nearby Summerleaze Gravel Pit. As they depart, they may well tell us what they think of us; *'crank crank crank'* they seem to say, and maybe they are right! A good corporate sulking day at the pit can present a veritable siege of ten or more, all hanging around to see who can look the most grumpy. That such a gangly-looking bird prefers to nest in the tops of trees is perhaps surprising, and that it also tends to nest in colonies, despite it's erstwhile lonesome behaviour, is also unexpected. If left undisturbed, heronries will continue to be used for decades, but in our fast-moving county, small groups move from site to site on a cyclical basis, with accompanying lack of breeding success. Nonetheless, the Cookhams would be impoverished without Jack and Moll to hand, so we can rejoice at every sighting.

Having mentioned the fields alongside Strand Water, particularly the large ones spanning over towards the Thames, they can be worth visiting late afternoon in winter, just before dusk. Dependent upon the nature and state of any winter crops, they are a favourite pre-roost feeding and conversation place for Lapwings and Starlings. The Lapwings will probably have been there most of the day picking out the leatherjackets and the like, their numbers gradually increasing as more move in to join the party. By dusk, some one thousand may have gathered. For the most part, they are content to wander around, occasionally lifting up to complete a circuit before re-alighting. As darkness approaches, the sky begins to fill with dark black clouds, eerily moving this way and that, coming in from all directions. When almost upon the spell-bound observer, the clouds transpire to be flocks of Starlings, swirling in the wind, each flock changing shape in mesmerising manner as the lead bird swings his entourage first left, then right, then upwards. Several of these flocks may then merge as ingredients in a soup of feathered frenzy, now with several hundred wheeling and whirling in formation.

Gaining a little height, an entire flock will circle once above a fancied landing place and then, as if by remote control, the entire bevy explodes downwards, each bird twisting and turning in exaggerated descent, whiffling one way, then the other, blanketing a piece of field like pastry laid over a pie. No sooner has one flock performed than another will group and the whole experience is re-played, complete with sound effects. Eventually, there may be two or three thousand Starlings feeding actively but, as each new group falls like torrents out of the sky, many on the ground will lift again and relocate to a quieter place, often causing Lapwings to join the swirl. The overall effect is like that of dancing waters, black against more black until, the scene played out, the Lapwings move off to Summerleaze and the Starlings to their unknown roost and the field is quiet again. This is not a regular occurrence by any means, but I have witnessed it several times at this location over the years. I hope you do too.

Returning to our stream-side walk, other delights still await our eager gaze. Noting each large tree along this linear woodland, one may perchance see a small mouse-like creature crawling up the bole of one of them;

mouse-like that is until it suddenly drops from the position gained and flies to the base of the next tree in the line. This will be a Treecreeper, aptly named and most diminutive in stature and personality. With faint *seeps*, it can be observed searching each crevice in the craggy barks of species such as Crack Willow, Chestnut, Ash or Oaks, being less at home on the smoother-barked trees. Indeed, Treecreepers even make their nest in tiny holes behind the bark. Seen closely, it will be observed to comprise a shrivelled Curlew, liberally mixed with Woodpecker, its needle-like down-curved bill steered with unerring precision by long-toed feet forming a tripod with its stiff tail.

Delicately marked with varying shades of brown, the back and wings are striated and barred with gentler, lighter hues. The underparts are a clean, creamy white and its tail has a darker band at its tip. It will gradually ascend a tree in spiral fashion until, tiring of its scenery, or suffering from vertigo, it will rapidly flit to the bottom of another and repeat the act. Though constantly active, it is a confiding bird and it might prove possible to watch one a few feet away, under which circumstances it will be worth keeping an eye out for a second bird, as they often move around in pairs. Then, as quickly as its presence was discerned, our tiny 'Wood-Picker' is gone, not to be seen again that day, as if it has melded with the tree-coat on which it was feeding.

---

JUNE
　　The seed that has died
　　Its new life can't hide.
　　Whilst chicks, life denied
　　In cruel talons ride.

　　　　Swifts screaming out, as if in pain
　　　　In between houses, and then back again.
　　　　Dunnocks stalk through hedgerow's ankles
　　　　And Corn Buntings trill, like car key jangles.

It can also be a gregarious bird and in the colder months will sign up with one of the numerous mixed feeding flocks that scour our hedges and woodlands for essential energy-giving food. Such flocks may well consist of Blue Tits, Great Tits, Long-tailed Tits, Coal Tits, Wrens, Dunnocks, Treecreepers and even the occasional Lesser Spotted Woodpecker. These multi-species groups are a joy to experience. It is impossible to watch without feeling embraced by the non-stop movement and the incessant contact calls of different stanza that surrounds the observer on a cold frosty morning in a quiet corner of Quarry Woods, or even Strand Lane.

Treecreepers are sedentary types, not taken to lengthy flights. A retiring bird, the male's spring time song is not often heard, comprising extremely high squeaks whispered to his nearby fiancee. The courtship dance is one of high-speed pursuit around the bases of trees and bushes, each occasionally stopping for a time of mutual wing-trembling, before setting off again on the magic roundabout chase. On a birding walk, every sound needs to be investigated. By such means are Treecreepers enabled to enthral.

Yet still the delights of this stretch of water are unquenched as encounters with various summer warblers are in prospect. The Blackcap is one, chauvinistically named, for the female has a rich chocolate cap instead. She is a skulking individual, only with certainty discovered when sharp *tzchak* calls emanate from the shrubs indicating we are too close to her chosen patch. The male, more often seen than his partner, is a Jekyll and 'Hide' character, being almost impossible to locate when issuing song from the depths of a shrub or bush but more

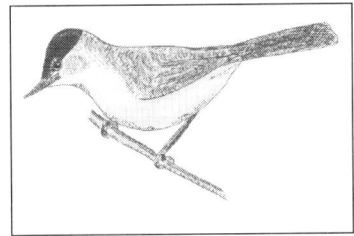
*Blackcap*

readily espied when feeding freely on the outer sprigs. His fine sooty cap placed on top of light grey and olive-brown upper plumage contrasts with lighter underparts. This fine songster comes to us in April, departing generally in October. However, we are living through a time of change for the species as more and more are visiting us during our winter time. This makes it difficult to differentiate between those that have celebrated Christmas-tide with us and those that nipped off for a tan whilst we froze.

It is in his song, however, that Mr Blackcap reveals his true nature. A fluty mélange of munificent notes uttered magnificently from his secret song-post, his five-second theme is repeated over and over again. Building up from a reluctant and scratchy beginning, he soon attains the mellifluous middle passages, moving quickly to the rising crescendo for which he is famed, and often called the Mock Nightingale. He also has a reputation for being something of a mimic of other bird songs. I have not detected this personally, although there is a perpetual similarity to the song of the Garden Warbler. A jerky, hurried flyer, he will quickly dash to another podium if disturbed, but will soon recommence his supper song, which he is content to recycle for hours on end.

In this same habitat, another warbler should be found, usually by the bird broadcasting his name from a suitable high perch. *Tchiff tchaff, tchiff tchaff, tchiff tchiff tchaff.* No marks for realising that this is a Chiffchaff, a bird that joins us in summer from African climes. Again, much like the Blackcap, large numbers are satisfied to stay here during our milder winters and it is quickly becoming a resident species. In appearance it is a yellowy-brown bird above and buff-white below, but with a prominent yellow stripe above the eye. Always active, it seems to feed at lower levels than those from which it sings. Unfortunately, without the accompanying song, one might not be too sure whether one is observing a Chiffchaff or a Willow Warbler. This latter bird overlaps with Chiffchaff in certain habitats and is generally similar, albeit being more olive-green above. Its song is significantly different being a descending and melancholy trill. Both may well be found around the Cookhams but perhaps the Chiffchaff is more plentiful. Two more right turns bring us back to Strand Lane whence we started.

It was in this area that my good friend Martin Gostling had one of his most 'Memorable Birding Moments'. The Gostlings live in Ingleborough, High Road which was built by Sparkes for Shirley's parents, the Farringtons, when they moved down from Macclesfield in 1961, and named it after a Yorkshire mountain. Shirley's earlier memories of childhood in the village include shopping for her mum at Mrs Mackie's shop at the corner of Graham Rd. Mrs Farrington was the last customer Mr Mackie had for his village delivery service. The shop was converted to a house for the Arnolds in the seventies. The first bird Shirley can remember recognising, having joined the Young Ornithologists Club, was a Linnet in Long Lane. Martin recalls an event that occurred along the stream-side footpath at the bottom of Strand Lane on a quiet day having noticed a flash of colour along the water just a few feet in front of him. He soon realised he was being welcomed by the local Kingfisher. Quite unperturbed by Martin's proximity, the Kingfisher wandered up and down a 15 yard stretch of water dipping at leisure for tiny Dace, upon success emerging to alight on an overhanging bough to deal the head of the unlucky fish a mighty blow or two on the branch before consuming it head first.

*Kingfisher*

Iridescent blues against sparkling broken water, glimpses of a deep royal chestnut belly and a dark stabbing bill make up this spectacular angler and they might be seen along the Thames or in the vicinity of small tributaries. They tend to feed well away from the nest site and I have seen them carrying food right across Widbrook Common and also on a regular airway over the tennis courts at Odney Club. The banks of the Thames around Cookham take the shape of wood and glass fibre hulls in summer, greatly reducing the opportunities for Kingfishers, but a few manage to find somewhere to dig their nest tunnels most years. A high pitched contact call is often the first indication of the presence of this artisan of air and water, not unlike that of the Dunnock, but deeper and more strident, befitting its more ebullient nature. They will hunt from perches above the water but are very adept at hovering for a few seconds over exposed stretches of stream to increase their hunting area. In this they resemble a large Humming Bird and are quite as colourful. Unlike Cormorants and other divers, they do not hunt their food under water. They will have already identified their prey before propelling themselves into the water to catch it, not wishing to get their plumage any wetter than necessary on wasted effort. Then, in a whirr of tiny, stiff-feathered wings, they carry it off to be dealt with in the customary manner. A huge percentage of our nation's Kingfishers perished in the fierce winter of 1891-92, and there have been other losses since, but with sensitive attention to our more rural areas, this emerald dirk will be with us well into the future.

*Fieldmouse*

But now perhaps it is time to leave this scenery to the fieldmouse and other rightful owners and move on to pastures new.

# Winter Hill

ONE STOP NEARER HEAVEN puts us atop the highest place in the Cookhams - Winter Hill. A plateau on the Chiltern escarpment, the Hill beckons with breath-taking views across the mighty Thames to the picturesque town of Marlow and the rising land of Buckinghamshire spread out below. This platform has witnessed Romans rampaging, Saxons sacking, Celts conquering, the meeting of Wessex and Mercian ideals, Danish and Norman fortification and a long list of kings and queens of England. The whole history of the Cookhams is known to this high-born part of our landscape. Today it is frequented by sweethearts, ramblers and picnicking families alike, most of them oblivious of what has gone before in the valley below.

The sharply-rising face of the hill is covered with shrubbery and hawthorn bushes and this is home to a variety of birds. Many an hour can be donated to a balmy day watching the world go by from this elevated platform. Chaffinches are probably the most numerous but one of the most striking would be another member of the same family, the Bullfinch. Arguably our most colourful finch, this thick-set bird may be encountered anywhere along the hillside and towards Cockmarsh, though rarely seen other than singly or in pairs. Both male and female possess velvet black caps, and grey backs, with black wing-tips barred with white. The female is light chestnut beneath whilst the male is a majestic crimson. Both exhibit a brilliant white rump in flight. For all this beautifying, it is a reclusive finch, preferring to make its life a mystery to the casual observer. On a dull, foggy morn, or a steamy evening in summer, one may hear the cock wooing his monogamous partner with a plaintive and piping *hoo hoo*, like a miniature owl. In the confines of the nest territory, the pair will converse with hushed parrot-like squeaks and chunterings. On the move, he leads the way from bush to bush, the hen following dutifully a few seconds later.

With so much cherry growing in Cookham over the years, Bullfinches (or Budfinches) doubtless fared well, their immensely powerful bill dealing effortlessly with the larger seeds and stones of fruit. In the past, when plums, cherries, currants and pears were grown in most gardens, allotments and park-lands, the effects of this fruit and flower-eating bird were not hard felt in any one locality, with no one tree succumbing to its attentiveness. Unfortunately, because fruit growing is nowadays a commercial undertaking, concentrated at particular locations, Bullfinches can gather in pest proportions and they are now legally controlled in such areas. With its beady black eye peering imperiously from its black-masked head, who are we to dislodge it from its position in the grand order of providence. Like the Hill itself, the Bullfinch is cloaked in our history and enthroned in our present. Hail the king of finches, say I. May its abundance be exceeded only by its beauty.

Another finch which can be found here is the Linnet, or Linnard, from its affection for linseed. Endemic to most of the area, this perky performer hardly sits still to be identified at all. Often in small groups, or family parties in summer-time, they may establish themselves on a prominent bush or be seen foraging on the ground. A tiny-billed specimen, attracted to smaller seeds such as found on teasels, it is overall a much daintier bird than the Budfinch. Captured in large numbers by our Victorian forebears, it proved a handsome cage bird, the male in a dashing summer uniform incorporating a speckled red breastplate, a matching helmet, a cape of varying browns and a steely grey-blue wing panel. A deeply forked tail brings up the rear. In winter, the chest and forehead are duller and more striated, resembling the browner female. At this time of year, huge flocks form to ease the task of finding good feeding, but the Linnet is still an individualistic bird and ones and two's will readily leave the main group to forage on their own, rejoining a little later, if the mood takes them. In April and May, a male will sometimes move surreptitiously away from his peers to set up a lonely vigil of song.

---

JULY
> Sky hazey
> Sun blazey
> Heat crazy
> Feel lazy.
>> Terns on the river
>> Kingfishers on the stream
>> Gambolling House Martins
>> A mid-summer's dream.

With deceptive variability, it will alternate rapidly from reedy chatterings to melodic strains, the whole scripted to captivate and bring the promise of summer to a cool dawn or a chilly evening. Captivated by their minstrelsy and closing ones eyes, the shimmering heath and gorse forests are brought to mind ahead of their time, as if transported by Tardis a few weeks into the future.

*"Linnard, Linnard, oiling the wings of time"*

Linnets often strike me as being somewhat unstructured in their behaviour, like restless children wondering what to get up to next. They will rush up to a roof-top, chatter for a while and then fly over to a nearby field for a spell. A few moments later, they are on the move again and may head for the top of a large tree a hundred yards away. Then they may descend to play in a hedgerow for a short period of time, soon lifting to return to the original garden some way off, constantly calling to each other with nasal notes. I am sure there is purpose to it all somewhere! On Winter Hill, they may be seen working their way along the rows of bushes on the slopes, or moving around the cornfields and stable-yards on the ridge. Although not regarded as a bird of domestic habitat, it is beneficial in gardens, hoovering up large numbers of grubs and caterpillars to feed four or five young, with a second brood following in good years. A ball of feathered delight for our delectation.

The elevated views from the top of the Hill facilitate the unusual experience of watching birds from above. House Martins and Swallows scythe their way beneath and Jays flop from end to end. Swans rise up toward us from the river below and Woodpigeons disperse in panic from a low level tree, clearly showing their air force markings on the top of their wings. But it is when one of the local Kestrels turn up that the fun begins. A pair of this delicately-marked falcon has resided along the top of the Hill for some years, often producing a family of four young. When all six birds are hunting together, it is an awesome spectacle. Birds of prey are normally silhouetted against the sky and plumage details are hard to discern, but viewed from above, such detail is plain to see. Both adults have a dark tan back and inner wing, blotched and spotted black. The primary wing feathers, and some of the secondary ones, are also black, making the outer half of the wing very dark. The females head is brown whilst the male's is ashy grey. It is the tail that aids separation most readily, the females being barred along its length, whereas the male's is slate grey without barring, though with a broad black band at the tip. Juveniles resemble the female, their wings initially being rounder at the tip until full grown.

The Kestrel is our most common bird of prey and also our most widespread, happy to eke out a living on farmland, open heaths, parks or waste ground. It is probably most associated with motorway verges, an extensive linear hunting ground provided for it courtesy of the Ministry of Transport! When perched, the bird has a peculiar hunched appearance. Hunting mainly for unsuspecting voles, Kestrels will also take small birds, especially during the breeding season with extra mouths to feed. They will add insects to their diet, often catching them in mid-air in their talons. Unlike the Hobby which does this too and then eats on the wing, the Kestrels I have seen catching insects have taken them to a perch to deal with. In spring, the male may be seen performing his courtship flight. This often takes the form of flying along with very shallow wingbeats in a sort of shiver-flight, or circling with the tail constantly fanned. Later in the year it is possible to see all six birds of a family hunting on the sculptured slopes of Winter Hill, the young soon getting the idea of hanging on the air, but taking much longer to work out what the objective of this behaviour is.

I well recall watching young Kestrels learning to hunt, this time along Strand Lane, where three young had been produced; one male and two females. The young buck was a real extrovert, invariably swooping low over my head when I made my appearance. On one occasion, having done this whilst I was on a raised bank, this impudent hawk commenced to hover at my eye height, just some ten to fifteen feet away. As if to prove his new-found skills, he suddenly plummeted to the ground and made a firm grasp to the back of the largest water vole I had ever seen. The rodent was easily half his size and readily dismissed the young offender from his rear. The incensed 'rat' then turned, raised himself on his hind legs and commenced to box the Kestrel with his front paws. In disguised confusion, the Kestrel began retaliation with his own feet, but quickly discovered an element of ineptitude when he fell flat on his back! The vole, in classic disdain, turned his back and ambled slowly off, not concerned in any way. Young master falcon, determined to make up for his blushes in front of his small audience, immediately righted himself and, in half flight, half run, launched himself yet again at the disappearing potential meal-turned aggressor. Fixing himself assuredly upon the upper surfaces of this retiring rodent, he squealed with glee.

Unfortunately this seemed only to fuel mister vole with extra determination to rid himself of this boring nuisance, and so, raising himself on all fours, he simply charged into the briars and nettles at the base of my observation post, ignominiously sweeping the bird from his shoulders. Yet again, the indignant Kestrel was portrayed flat on his back a few feet beneath me. You never have a camera with you when you want one, do you! I presumed by now he was quite spent and would simply lope off and sulk somewhere, but I had underestimated the character of this bird. With hardly a backward glance, he swiftly rose to the hover right in front of my eyes again and after just a few seconds, swooped once more, to almost the same spot, this time emerging clutching a much more sensible sized meal, a small field-mouse probably. In obvious boastful fashion he rose again to hover a few feet in front of me, dangling his snack beneath him to be sure I could see it. Then, with triumphal flair, he carried it off to an unseen picnic bench to consume his well-earned meal. This sequence all transpired in perhaps a few seconds but seemed an age in its unravelling and it was as if both he and I were learning in class together.

*The Fight!*

Viewing families of Kestrels on Winter Hill is usually only possible until July, thereafter the young being encouraged to disperse, distances getting further each day over a few weeks until they may be only rarely seen in their original territory, having to wait until the following spring to attain adult plumage and commence their own romancing. The adults meanwhile remain holding their territory for their lifetime which seems, from research, to be some three to four years. Longevity amongst our feathered friends is measured on a different scale from our own, and fully reflects the nature of their environment and the dangers of predators – including man. A general rule is that the larger the bird, the longer it lives. Small passerines, plagued by cats and raptors, may only survive two or three years, most young unfortunately perishing in their first year. That is why breeding pairs annually produce something like six to ten young on average, simply to maintain the population in each year. Swans on the other hand can live well into double figures. One ringed individual was recorded at Sir Peter Scott's Wildfowl Reserve at Slimbridge as migrating every winter from Russia for 21 years.

Mute Swans gather together at the end of the breeding season and, from the lofty gallery of Winter Hill, a lamentation of these majestic birds may be seen on the Thames or the gravel pits beyond. Sometimes they come across to the fields at the bottom of the slope to graze or to loaf, their waddling action looking even more exaggerated from above. Often, flocks of geese adopt these fields after cropping to consume the gleanings. Usually they are Canada Geese, but occasionally Greylag Geese join in. The Canada Goose is not an indigenous species in these islands but was introduced as an ornamental addition to parks and gardens in the eighteenth century. Like most introduced species, it quickly established itself the length and breadth of the land and can now be seen in huge numbers in our area. I once sat beneath a hedge near Summerleaze Pit at dusk as the Canadians returned in skeins from their feeding near Long Lane and had counted one thousand and fifty before the Lamberts lost their hold and I could only guess how many were in each subsequent honking group. I suspect that local farmers took appropriate action at that time as there have only been one to two hundred since.

*Canada Goose*

Stepping back off the ridge, and exploring some of the footpaths through the fields on the plateau of the Hill can also be rewarding. The village beyond rests under a 'cloud of verdure' whilst in the paddocks, arable fields and set-aside areas in the foreground, a mixture of species can be expected. The mature hedgerows which salute the pleasant lanes are home to many a party of Greenfinches, their rusty-hinge calls rasping through summer and winter alike. Dunnocks skulk around the legs of the hedge, occasionally nipping out onto the road, peering back into the hedge, and swiftly disappearing once more. Often known as the Hedge Sparrow, this bird is not a sparrow at all, as a glimpse of its thin insectivorous bill will assert. Officially a Hedge Accentor, Dunnock will do fine as a name she will recognise, but over the centuries her mail will have been addressed to "Dykie", "Hatcher", "Hedge Jug" or "Hedge Pick". All of these adequately describe the habits of this attractive but retiring bird. Her dark grey head and chest outlines her beady black eye which peers out from a brown ear patch. (Birds have their ears behind and below the eye, usually covered with feathers which are distinctly coloured, forming a patch of contrast). The mottled brown back is excellent camouflage for a shy species and yet this frequenter of the hedgerow's dungeons of darkness possesses a song that evinces a true spirit of lightness. Often projected from an unseen stage, a fluty trill breaks through the gloom to fill the lane and echo from the fences. The song has a haunting quality, beautiful yet constrained, as if from an opera singer confined to the tower. Not dissimilar to the song of the Wren, it has none of the harshness or scalding rattle, for this princess of singers wishes to allure, whilst maintaining her mystery.

Adjacent to the golf links at this level is a meadow which has often been left as set-aside for some while. Home to Skylarks and Meadow Pipits, it has produced some of my most 'Memorable Birding Moments'. One in particular I have not seen elsewhere and occurred late one summer's evening when I was passing through this field to watch the river below, where the Little Egret had been reported coming to roost earlier that week. I found myself distracted from this task by a sudden build up of Black-headed Gulls over the field. Gulls return inland from end of June onwards and so the quantity, soon around five hundred, was not surprising in itself, but the effective way they began hovering above the mature trees along the ridge drew my attention. I soon realised they were picking out the Cockchafers as they emerged just before dusk. Hundreds seemed to be consumed in a frenzy of hover-hunting.

Having seen flocks of gulls gorging themselves on flying ants in season, this in itself was not too unusual. However, I next became aware of increasing numbers of these gulls descending low over the field and very purposefully quartering the meadow from one end to the other and back again, like a ghostly white blanket. In fading light, there were soon several hundred following each other in waves across this field, just a few inches above the crop of grasses and weeds. After closer observation I realised that the front line of gulls were disturbing small insects from the plants just beneath their wings. The following group would quickly take any that popped up in front of them, only to resume their low level activity to the benefit of the ones following behind them. And so this was repeated for several minutes before dark, when the entire ensemble retired to the adjacent links for a spot of preening before setting off for their west London roost.

This somewhat sacrificial form of feeding, one bird creating opportunity for others, I had not witnessed previously. In fact gulls are well known for harrying each other to steal what they can. The story does not end there, as I returned with my friend Martin Gostling the following evening and saw the play unfold yet again, but this time we noticed that this very effective means of putting up large numbers of insects had not gone unnoticed. Amongst the fading white and grey shapes, we suddenly noted a darker bird, and then another, and yet another. These darker shapes were swifter, more mobile, and working above the main flock. We soon realised that a number of raptors had been attracted to the feast. In the last moments of darkness we were entertained by two adult Hobbies, with one of their offspring, and an adult Kestrel with four youngsters learning the ropes. As a lesson in opportunism, it was interesting enough, but to be amongst such a large number of birds, with so much activity and variety of hunting techniques laid out before us was a memorable occasion. The following evening was less warm and the gulls hardly bothered, but the Hobbies were there again and provided their own spectacle. The following day, the field was mown, ending the spectacle for at least another season. However, this same field has also produced the largest mutation of thrushes I have ever encountered; 37 Mistles feeding together beneath the watchful eye of the Hobby.

Resembling a small and compact Peregrine Falcon, the Hobby is a summer visitor to this country. About the size of the Kestrel, this dashing bird of prey is dark slate grey above and speckled beneath, the male having striking crimson plumage around the legs and undertail area, whilst the female is mottled buff below.

*Hobby chasing House Martin*

Both birds have a dramatic black mask giving them a Lone Ranger appearance, somewhat like the Wheatear. And indeed, they are most usually seen alone, but once the young have left the nest, the adult pair will work together more frequently. Renowned for their aerial agility, chasing Martins and Swifts affords exhilarating watching. With an ability to set their wings into a typical scythe shape, they gradually ascend into a whirling mass of hirundines, who all too late realise what has happened;

by which time the predator has set his eyes upon a likely dish and set off in pursuit with huge energy and determination. Success rates are varied, dependent on the element of surprise achieved.

Another technique appears to require two birds working in partnership. I have seen the male fly slowly and purposefully into full view of a flock of Martins or Starlings. Whilst he soared majestically around, at quite low level, I spotted his partner gliding in from some distance and height. Wings set in anhedral, and without a flap to attract attention, the second bird was soon amongst the unsuspecting passerines, causing great confusion. Having failed a catch on this occasion, they both soared effortlessly from the turmoil, upwards until out of sight, to discuss perhaps their next campaign on the wing or make plans for the continuing search for their purpose.

*"No bird of prey knows the hidden path*
*no Falcon's eye has seen it"*
*Job 28:7*

On yet a further occasion, I found myself observing another hunting technique of which I am convinced I was made a part. I had been watching a Hobby working amongst Martins for some time with binoculars, the bird eventually gaining great height, straight into the sun, at which point I dropped my arms to rest them. I had been aware of causing some disturbance for a Sedge Warbler which had been popping up and down in a bush to scold me whilst I was absorbed with the Hobby. No sooner had I dropped my arms and was squinting to clear my eyes from sun glare when I both felt and heard a bird swooping just behind my neck. I had but a moment to turn and see the Hobby righting itself a few inches off the ground having stooped from its great height onto this unsuspecting warbler, using me, I am convinced, as it's 'beater'. I have experienced this many a time with Sparrowhawks, which will suddenly flash over your shoulder as you walk down an enclosed lane, knowing that you will automatically cause small birds to take flight. However, this was the first time I had been 'used' in this way by a Hobby, and it was certainly the closest I have ever been to this magnificent hunter of the air.

The bird is not always so frenetic in its hunting, however, and one can sit in wonderment as a Hobby hawks for insects on a still balmy eve, watching him pluck a suitable bug out of the air in his talons. Then, in rigid wings, the feet are drawn forward to the bill and the inedible bits such as legs, shells or wings are daintily removed and left to flutter to the ground, the dismembered morsel eventually disappearing down its throat. A bird may well feed like this for an hour or so if left undisturbed and often at such an altitude that it is impossible to see what is happening without those binoculars I recommended you to carry!

Any of the meadows nearby can hold creatures of interest. A covey of Grey Partridges strut around them, a choking call the first indication of their presence. A huske of Hares may be found and a nye of Pheasants 'cough' to each other from corner to corner. Quail have been heard up here too, but many a slip is waiting to be made as far as bird calls are concerned in this area. Strange noises often emanate from the grounds of Winter Hill Farm, owned by John Copas. John has been a keen collector of game-birds and waterfowl for some years and has amassed a varied collection of unusual and ornamental species. Amongst the geese present are Red-breasted, White-fronted, and Bar-headed types. Carolina Wood Ducks, Marbled Teal and Red-crested Pochard are often joined by Mandarin flying in from the Thames. Shelduck waddle around the pool edge and Guinea Fowl roam the surrounding field, anxiously watchful for marauding Foxes.

Next door live the family Mercer, David and Julia, second generation General Practitioners to the community. David's father, Dr Vaudrey Mercer, was another notable bird watcher in the village during the forties, being extremely interested in bird song. He would often give talks on the subject to local groups. This then is Winter Hill, with its bluebells and buttercups; grasses growing effortlessly up the steep slopes; romping rabbits and bouncing butterflies; the valley below teeming with life. Can there be a prettier place?

*Kestrel over Winter Hill*

# The Rise

THE TWO THINGS THAT BRING PEOPLE to places are prosperity and attractiveness. For such reasons the Rise was born, growing outwards from the railway station, first in fits and starts, then in more hurried fashion, the areas between sparse cottages soon being filled with newer houses. During WW1, the population was swelled with evaccuees from London and some, like Sidney Jewell, who was 7 when 'escaping' to Cookham in 1916, are still here. Meadow-land and commons soon succumbed to the need for housing and this part of the village became transformed. The large spaces between the cottages built along High Road and Lower Road in the mid nineteenth century have been filled in with progressively more modern designs. From the station to the school, most of High Road was allotments, with wheat fields beyond them, overlooked by such premises as Prospect Cottage built in 1860. The twin-track railway has been replaced with a single track, and the traditional crossing gate modernised with sirens and flashing lights. The little wooden shop built by Mr Sayells as a newsagents around 1914 has since been owned by Mr Groves and Mr Akrill. It is now a shoe repair business, owned by Mr Stokes since 1962, and named Reliance after the well-known insurance company of that name, Mr Stokes' former employer.

Anne Keating has many memories of the growth of the area. Born in the village in 1911, her father knew many of the incumbents as he was a local gardener, and caretaker at Moor Cottage before it became a nursing home. Anne grew up as the village grew alongside her. She remembers Cooper's Store becoming a Budgen's, the brick-built bridge on the Moor provided by Mrs Balfour Allen, and the opening of the Memorial Stone by Mr Wallace. She recalls the naming of Worster Road after one of the residents there, Mr Worster. Little has changed along this road, apart from the new style house owned by Nigel and Elisabeth Sanders. The corner house was once occupied by Stanley Spencer, but Anne remembers Miss Stephens who lived there before. Nearby was a fish shop and opposite the school was a small dairy. The shops near Pinder Hall many years ago were Hollands, then the poultry shop owned by Mr Barge, Mr King the cobblers and Shackels, the 'Thistle' laundry. She recalls the names even now through a rhyme she learnt as a child "Mr Shackel went to Holland in a Barge to see the King". Anne worked at Herries School until she was seventy years old

The site on which Pinder Hall now proudly stands was a builders yard owned by Mr Wakelin, after whom Wakelins End was named, once built upon his land. He was renowned for falling off his bicycle after sampling the local brew. The present caretakers to Pinder Hall, Richard and Hazel Probert, live in Bank House, so called because of the Lloyds Bank that used to be adjacent. Opposite was Rise Autos, the garage and filling station, long since demolished. Anne's husband Mick once owned the garage before moving to Station Garage as a driver of limousines for the landed gentry and corporate magnates travelling to London. The high archway into the site was designed as such to facilitate the coach and horses that originally provided this service. Pete Dutfield rented the yard until eventually taking over the site to enhance his excellent motor mending ministration to the community.

AUGUST
The farmer has whistled
The fields are left thin
But the Masters own harvest
Is not fully in.

Dragonflies dodging sharp Hobby's claws
Midges enveloped in Swifts gaping jaws.
Crows all debating with self-righteous 'caws',
And young garden birds in pussy cat's paws!

A notable building in this part of the Cookhams is Elizabeth House. Known by this name since 1980, it was originally built as the village police station in 1910 and was scheduled for demolition when police coverage was regionalised and resident Bobbies became a thing of the past. However, a group of local folk, led by Elisabeth Sanders, championed the cause of retaining the building as a Day Centre. After much hard work and fund raising, the group won the day and the facility was commissioned in 1980, on the eightieth birthday of Her Majesty Queen Elizabeth the Queen Mother, after whom it was named. It was opened by Richard Baker and dedicated in 1981 by Rev Grover. Today it provides a valuable meeting place where elderly Cookhamites enjoy fellowship, swap yarns and eat together on a daily basis.

Doll Cooper too has many memories of her childhood and working career in the village. Her parents Joseph and Rhoda Grimsdale, moved to Bob Caught's farm in Cookham Dean from Bisham when Doll was just six years old. Joseph was one of 10 brothers and sisters and daughter Doll herself became one of five siblings (Ted, Den, Doll, Joe and Betty). Doll would walk from the Dean to school at Holy Trinity every day, until Jack Chastall started a local bus service through the village. In those days, Sawfords garage was a small school, prior to the 'new' one opened by Mrs Lewis. Doll remembers her first job, scrubbing the flagstones and floors at the Beech Bowls and walking to Marlow regularly for stockings and the like, all for 12/- per week. She also worked for Sir James and Lady Boyton at Fratons. In 1949, having married Bill Cooper, the couple then moved to the Rise and subsequently took one of the Dean Cottages in Whyteladyes Lane. The properties in the Lane in those days were all named, such as the house that belonged to my wife's mum and dad, Mayfrey (mum's Christian name followed by the end of father's surname, Godfrey). It was not until the 1970's that the Post Office decided that sequential numbering had become necessary to overcome numerous wrong deliveries. Today's mortgage holders would be pleased to reserve a house such as Mayfrey for the £5 deposit that John and May had to find in 1935! In later years, Doll became one of the local post delivery ladies and came to know village and villagers alike.

Much of the Rise is dominated by the two large gas holders constructed in recent years, despite an attempt to conceal them behind a row of Poplar trees which at last reached a similar height to the tanks in 1996, only to be cut down as potentially unsafe! I've called them Bill and Ben as they resemble upturned flower-pots when full. Being a gas holder is an up and down experience but despite being the only vertically mobile buildings in the Cookhams, birds seem quite content to roost around the rim of the framework every night. The oldest tank, Bill, was constructed in 1925 whilst Ben when not installed until 1967. Bill holds half a million cubic feet of gas, whilst Ben is twice the size. Bill climbs up and down inside a frame whilst Ben spirals up and down without such support. Together they supplement the mains supply to Cookham's population mainly during the winter months. Once empty, they take seven hours to refill. They are somewhat like chameleons; following a fresh lick of green paint every eight years or so, they gradually change colour through a range of browns to rusty orange, at which time the brushes come out again, plastering 2600 litres onto Bill and 3500 litres onto Ben. Unseen on the inside of the holders, a heaving mass of molecules hustle around at over 1000 miles per hour, colliding randomly with each other and expanding to fill the available space. Just a sugar-lump cube of gas might contain 30 million million million molecules rushing this way and that waiting their turn to be squirted down the pipe to our cooker or heater. Isn't it amazing how much is going on inside something you can't even see!

Bill & Ben

Recent years have witnessed other changes around the Rise. In the early nineties, work was carried out to overcome the regular flooding which occurred after heavy rainwater washing down from the farmland stretching up towards the Dean. Major disruption lasted for many months as the Lower Road and High Street were excavated to an enormous depth and huge drainage pipes installed. In 1994, street lighting was introduced along the Lower Road for the first time, although only 10 lights were permitted. However, within twelve months they had bred and their offspring had established territory along Whyteladyes Lane. In 1995, more major work was carried out to divert sewage pipes to an adjacent treatment works, which will eventually mean the closure of the Cookham sewage farm. In the same year, another first-time event occurred with the overnight appearance of Cookham's first mini-roundabout, installed at the junction of The Pound and Maidenhead Road, opposite the Gate Public House, itself re-named The Old Anchor Inn at around the same time, whilst the Railway Tavern was refurbished and re-opened as The Cookham Tavern.

Even whilst the community was still reeling under these projects, the Electricity Company arrived to replace the numerous small overhead cables with a new installation involving some heavier duty cables. It was interesting to note that the birds which used to adopt the wires as viewing perches took several days before getting accustomed to the thicker replacements. Unfortunately, the work did not prevent a tragedy when a small crane lorry made contact with some of the remaining open wires causing the lorry to explode into flame with fatal results to the crew. During much of this activity, the summer of 1995 had been one of the longest, hottest and driest spells for decades and inevitably outdoor fires occurred, the most memorable one scorching the whole area between Maidenhead Road and Strand Lane, with flames up to twelve feet high. The Fire Brigade called in eight appliances from as far afield as Wargrave. Amazingly, by the end of the year, the tips of the brassica crop subsequently planted were pushing through. This, and many other calls upon the Cookham Part Time crew convinced the authorities to cancel plans to close the station as a cost cutting exercise.

The roll call of local men who have manned this station reflects the family names of the community through the generations. The station was first established in 1889, and it has always been manned by volunteers. In those earlier days, the 'appliance' was a steam-driven pump, towed around by horse. In these times of automatic 999 services, and appliances careering out of the door within a few minutes of the call, the days of nags and nutty slack seem a creation ago. In that bygone era, the first volunteer to respond to the alarm had a well-practised ritual to perform. "First catch your horse", the manual would say. "Next, establish good fire under pump boiler to generate steam" it would continue. Meanwhile, this chap, or the next to arrive, would run or cycle from house to house to rouse the rest of the crew. Eventually, horse and men would be on their way to the incident, all ready to record the oft-used report phrase - 'Premises well alight on arrival!!'

Over the years these brave men have had to protect a gradually increasing number of properties in the Cookhams. Of the more recent generations, John Webb reflects on a 34-year term of service commencing in 1954. John was a joiner by trade, working at Hardings in Halldore Hill, having been born in Purley and finding himself in Cookham in 1934 when his father moved here to work as chauffeur to Joe Allen who owned Dial Close in those days. John married Bridey in 1952, a few years after she arrived from Kerry and they moved into Day Dawn in Whyteladyes Lane, just a few doors from my wife's father, John Godfrey, with whom John worked on many a carpentry project in the village. Service in the local brigade has been very much a family affair over the years. John's brother Charlie served for 14 years before being invalided out through injury on active duty. David Matthews, the village smithy, followed in his father's footsteps and the current Station Officer, Mervyn Dodd, follows the traditions of his father Bert and grand-father Harry. Tom Quelch, who was born at Whiteplace Farm where his father worked for Lord Astor, served for more than 33 years and now lives in Broomhill with his wife Charlotte.

John remembers rescuing horses that had strolled over swimming pool covers (that were always conveniently green in those days!), numerous chimney fires in the era of coal burning and battling with Tony Blackburn's thatch. He recalls the heath fire that crept underground after being extinguished above, and set fire to the appliance some yard away whilst no-one was looking. They had to requisition another one on return to base! Yet another recollection of John's is the 'Memorable Birding Moment' when he was head-butted by a Robin in his workshop, prior to discovering a nest with young, in between some old paint tins. However, they eventually got on better together until the young left and peace was restored to the Rise.

With all the bricks and mortar that have been planted over the decades, it is perhaps surprising that any birdlife could be found, but maturing gardens and hedges have lured a wide range of garden birds into the Rise. Farmland Linnets may nest in adjacent gardens and flocks of House Sparrows ply from roof-tops to field edges for food. Enormous numbers of Starlings use the huge green gas-holders as a roost, alternate black and brown silhouettes as the young join the adults in late summer. Collared Doves bill and coo in garden fruit trees, ignoring the barbecue brigade below, whilst Goldfinches twitter above the sound of lawn mowers and ghetto blasters. Bird tables are visited with relish and nest boxes quickly inhabited (provided they are mounted with the hole facing north to avoid

*Reed Bunting*

direct sunshine). Winter food stations may be visited by Brambling or Yellowhammers. I've even had Reed Buntings on mine, and Siskins just love those red bags of peanuts.

We tend to overlook the more domesticated birds. When did you last take a good look at a Starling, for example. Close examination will reveal one of the most striking plumages of our indigenous species. The male is covered with dark iridescent feathers which change colour with the angle of the light, now green, then black, then silver. There is great variability between individuals and, depending on the season and age of the bird, it might look all brown, all dark, or a combination of the two. The huge bill may be bright yellow or dark grey and the legs a dull brown or bright red. They are boisterous and full of 'street cred' but their song belies a gentler spirit. When a murmuration of some hundred gather on the local gas holder, a cacophony of noise results. A series of clicks, croaks, whistles and sub-notes are all strung together in a wide variety: never beautiful, but always creative. A great mimic, all sorts of other species are heard as a male Starling gives forth from a prominent chimney pot. I've heard Kestrel, Cuckoo, Little Owl, Coot, Blackbird, Jay and even Wigeon issue from this wizard of mimicry. At roost, the ensemble is too noisy and raucous to pick out any individual as they all seem to talk to each other at the same time. It does not seem mandatory for any bird to listen; just to make a noise. That is until the local Sparrowhawk hoves into view, then silence quickly ensues.

Interaction between Starlings and Sparrowhawks is interesting. We have all seen groups of Starlings flying over on a purposeful journey to an open piece of land for feeding, chuckling contentedly to each other at the thought of the feast awaiting them. Straight and level flight, obviously with pre-planning. We are also familiar with the whirling masses of them on a pre-roost dance in the skies, wheeling aimlessly in clouds of differing shapes, each bird tucked tightly into the next, making the whole gathering appear as a noisy plume of smoke borne on the wind. Quite possibly, we will have seen the aerobatic agility of the Starling as groups of them feed on hoards of flying ants in random individualistic fashion. But every now and again, Starlings will be seen to silently form up into a flat, wide spaced formation, the whole squadron circling at the same level, possibly several groups of fifty to one hundred birds. This is the time to scan the sky because they will have already seen something that puts dread into each of their hearts - the Sparrowhawk. We often like to think that our birds of prey would not really harm another bird, relying on carrion to live on. Let there be no such misconception about this hawk. It is a purposeful and tenacious predator, perfectly equipped with every tool needed for an efficient hunting life-style with a licence to kill from its Maker.

Sparrowhawks often hunt over the Rise, knowing that each small garden attracts birds to feeding tables and to the mature foliage on hand. The tall 'privacy' hedges and even the houses themselves afford every opportunity for surprising unsuspecting spadgers and throstles, and especially Starlings. There's nothing a cock hawk likes to serve his mate more than leg of Sparrow or breast of Blue Tit. Wafting down from the tree-line above Bradcutts Lane (which used to be called Roses Lane), or across the fields behind Whyteladyes Lane, this expert huntsman will fly along in front of the houses, below roof height and then suddenly dash through the gap between two of them to appear magically and instantaneously above an innocent feeding party of garden birds. A gap regularly used for this type of attack is the one between my own house and my neighbours, Sam and Patricia Woods. Smaller creatures than ourselves have much less distance for brain signals to travel and convert commands into physical action. Within an instant of appearing over our garden, the hawk will have checked every bit of ground and every perching position, noted the food items on display, picked the most tasty looking morsel and be heading towards it at 50 miles per hour before being seen by anything (except me!).

If there happens to be nothing in the first supermarket, he instantly converts his dash to another technique. Picking a mature hedge ahead, he will keep below the top until the last moment and suddenly rise over its peak, his frightening silhouette putting up every bird on the other side, one of which he will single out for pursuit. This method has been called the 'boo' technique, and even as I work on this paragraph, a fine female has just employed this tactic right outside our patio door, rewarded with a hapless House Sparrow. Yet another strategy is the high soaring approach. Often no more than a speck in the sky, the hawks amazing vision enables it to pick out prey several hundred feet below, maybe a vole or a small bird. Getting gradually lower to finally pinpoint his target, the hawk will instantaneously flap his powerful wings once at the commencement of a dive, fold his wings closely at the side of his body and head straight for his victim. This is never a vertical dive, as would be the case of a Kestrel dropping for an item over which he had hovered. This is an angled dive, indicating that the Sparrowhawk was looking to one side when up among the clouds, not vertically downwards. Reaching speeds of eighty to one hundred miles per hour, the hawk is quickly within talon range of his unsuspecting take-away.

This technique is usually reserved for more open country and I have not seen this 'stoop' method applied in hunting over the Rise. However, the dramatic stoop itself can be seen over the area during courting times. The male uses this ploy to both establish his territory and to attract his mate. After an exaggerated climb to great height, as if to get final inspiration from above, the male will stoop swiftly, sometimes injecting an extra flap or two just to maximise speed on the way down. When it looks as if the poor female is about to be knocked out of the tree, every flight surface available is mobilised and the male turns 80 mph downwards into 30 mph upwards in no more than three feet. An incredible spectacle to see, but only possible if you spend at least some time looking upward during walks! If you do, you may also see another Sparrowhawk courting routine. Firstly the male makes a catch of something he would like to give to his fancy-lady. If there happens to be no boxes of Black Magic flying around, then a Sparrow or House Martin will suffice. The female, having observed the hunt from a neutral tree, suddenly appears and starts to circle above the male. Both will then gradually circle higher and higher until a point is reached when the male flies in closely beneath the female, turns upside down and passes the food parcel to her outstretched talons. As she departs with it, the male, with a rush of blood to his head, has a final flourish before disappearing for a time of self-congratulation. Hazel and I have watched this routine even over the railway station on a busy shopping day. I'm sure everybody wondered what on earth we were watching up there. If only they knew!

> *"Does the hawk take flight by our wisdom,*
> *And spread his wings towards the south.*
> *Does the eagle soar at our command*
> *And build his nest on high?"*
> *Job 39:26*

Once there are young to be fed, time for cat and mouse games become limited and more direct methods have to be employed. Apart from taking young birds and squirrels from their respective nests, and singling out recently fledged youngsters who cannot yet fly properly, Sparrowhawks will take what seem to be incredible risks to get a meal. In a previous house I owned, there was a very substantial hedge on one side, eight feet high and six feet deep, with very dense growth in the middle and in which I grew large numbers of blackberries and raspberries. To me the hedge appeared impenetrable.

One day I saw all the small birds quickly flee to this hedge for protection and I guessed a hawk was about. From the vantage point of a bedroom window I saw the Sparrowhawk charge across the garden at full speed, close its wings and dive straight into the densest part of the hedge without deceleration. The bird literally head-butted a Sparrow right through the hedge and into mid air on the other side. Before the Sparrow lost any height in its trajectory, the Sparrowhawk came beneath it, inverted, grasped the squealing spadger from below, righted himself and swooped out of sight at the same speed he had arrived. All this probably took one and a half seconds, but during that time I was left to marvel at the incredible abilities of birds of prey to fling themselves headlong into hedges and undergrowth without harming themselves.

Only 30 years ago, the Sparrowhawk had been reduced to near rarity by a combination of pesticides and persecution. A more enlightened approach to the use of this particular chemical on farmland has resulted in their numbers being almost totally restored today.

There is another species of bird quick to alert all and sundry at the appearance of a Sparrowhawk, and that is the House Martin (presumably a Tent Martin in Adam's day!). Always on the wing, they are perpetually on the lookout and the first to detect one will utter a distinctive alarm call that brings an entire flock together to head towards the hawk and monitor its progress. They will not mob the bird as such; just keep tabs on it so they can be sure when it has left their territory. House Martins are colonial birds, returning each year to their favourite housing estate to re-use, or rebuild their mud and spittle holiday homes. I wonder what they *were* called before houses were invented? By mid-May the first eggs will have been laid and even hatched for the earlier arrivals. Others seem to delay their nesting activities for a couple of weeks, perhaps waiting to see how the weather will turn out or perhaps needing more time to regain body weight lost on their migration flight from Africa. During this time, several hundred can be found feeding off the slopes of Winter Hill.

The Broomhill colony usually consists of around thirty pairs. Many seem to build half a nest and then abandon it. Perhaps they go on to construct another down the road, or perhaps they are first-year birds, lacking the skills to complete the task. Either way, we seem to get about the same number each year, which of course, by the end of a second brood, may well be over 200 birds. Second broods are always a risky business. Our autumn weather is noted for its unpredictability and often, conditions have deteriorated before the second batch of young are fully fledged. The adults press on as long as they can, trying to get the young strong enough for their first flight, which may well be several thousand miles long! They do not always succeed, having to abandon the nest and young when the final summoning of Africa comes to them. However, I believe there are far more successes than disasters, especially as evidently the young from the first brood will help with the feeding of their younger brothers and sisters. I doubt this happens extensively amongst other species.

Ever gregarious, 'Martlets' feed on the wing in frantic, sweeping groups. Even when the whole colony gathers together for their nightly pre-roost barn dance, the pairings of males and females can usually be picked out. This gets more difficult when first brood youngsters join in, but with careful watching, it is possible to identify family groups moving around in the midst of the throng. In these late-evening performances, the entire assembly move together from one end of the territory to the other, but never seems to move out of the confines of the colony boundary.

## SEPTEMBER

The river banks of plastic, fibre glass and wood,
Will soon return to normal, which must be pretty good.
And PYO will be for apple, sweetcorn and for spud,
Before the banks of Cookham become a sea of mud.

>Cuckoos gone on holiday,
>Soon the rest will follow.
>Garden Warbler, Quail and Whitethroat,
>Turtle Dove and Swallow.

The air above one's garden will be silent one minute then bursting with '*threep*'s' the next. Every 10 minutes or so, a particular group becomes more vociferous and all the other birds gather around them, spiralling upwards to several hundred feet, becoming small dots high up in the darkening sky. After a short while, they break up and descend for a time of swooping up to their nests, and then disperse, the whole process repeated a little later. At a particular light level, quite suddenly, heaven calls for silence and they seem to have spirited themselves away for the night.

Another regular visitor to the Rise is the Tawny Owl. This tubby owl with its baleful expression was once far more common in the Cookhams but has suffered the consequences of ongoing development. However, those that remain like to examine the more mature gardens and perch in the older, stouter trees. Not that trees form the only acceptable perch by any means. I have watched one closely on the telegraph pole outside my house, on the power wires behind the house where Mr and Mrs Godfrey lived (now belonging to the Campbells), and observed one on the Bysshe's TV aerial, next to the Gostlings. On another occasion, a Tawny and I shared a roost for some twenty minutes at ten feet separation until I simply had to go, disturbing my new-found companion in the process. It is hard to estimate how many pairs may frequent the Cookhams, as they probably travel around the district somewhat, but from observations in Long Lane, the Rise, Quarry Wood, Winter Hill and Strande Water, maybe three or four pairs hold territory, with occasional forays from outside visitors.

Essentially a nocturnal hunter, birds will emerge just before dusk and become quite vocal. No single bird is responsible for the traditional tuwhit tuwhoo call. In fact, male and female combine to create this illusion. The female begins the conversation with a '*kuvitt*' call, immediately responded to by the male uttering his '*wehoo*', in perfect pitch and timing. The male, having thus responded, will often relocate to another perch for his next reply, thereby establishing his territory at the same time. When perched in enough light for clear viewing, and wings folded, the Tawny Owl looks generally brown above, with much flecking. The underwing is much lighter with numerous bands across the

*Juvenile Tawny Owl*

length of the wing and at the tips. Its round, haunting visage is highlighted by its enormous black eyes, both on the front of the face, as it is with most predators. Nesting starts in late winter in order that the young will be fledged as numbers of rodents are building up. By springtime, the fluffy, inquisitive young are crawling around on the woodland floor, sometimes straying onto roadside verges, looking pretty pathetic and in need of help. In fact, help is not needed nor should it be offered. Owlets have an incredible propensity for climbing back up the tree they have dropped from, quite unaided and are far more effective in sating their own appetites themselves than we humans could. So if one is found, please leave it to its parents to look after it; they do so all the way through to September!

Tawny Owls are also dressed to kill, with special feathers which differ from other bird forms. A feather is a wonderful piece of design (not, as some purport, the result of fraying on lizard's scales), having a central shaft on which a very precise number of barbs project from each side. Along the length each of these barbs are microscopic hooks on one side and loops on the other. These hooks and loops join together to keep the barbs parallel with each other for the full length of the feather. It was from this design that the familiar Velcro material was developed. An additional feature on the owl's feather is that the upper surface is covered with velvet-like coating of a myriad soft filaments, aiding silent flight on approach to his victim. Not that this makes the Tawny completely silent. I have become aware of the proximity of a Tawny at dusk at the bottom of Gibraltar Lane, only because I heard its wings passing just two or three feet above my head. Then, being able to see it alight in a stout tree a few yards away, I sat down on the road and we watched each other for fifteen minutes before more pressing business called the Tawny away. It is possible that the owl can control the amount of noise the wing makes, forsaking more efficient flight for silence in the final approach. The area of an owls wing, in proportion to its body size, is in any case much greater than many other birds, so its wingbeats can be less frequent, further reducing noise in flight.

Owls are the subject of mystery and folklore. Their eerie calls in the winter night, their ghostly fleeting appearance at dusk, sweeping menacingly across the glade and a silhouette full of foreboding. Expressionless eyes matched with a fearsome bill and cruel talons respond to every rustle in a fog-bound woodland. Little surprise that Shakespeare wrote, in *Love's Labour's Lost*:

> *When icicles hang by the wall*
> *And Dick the shepherd blows his nail*
> *And Tom bears logs into the hall*
> *And milk comes frozen home in pail*
> *When blood is nipped and ways be foul*
> *Then nightly sings the staring owl*
> *Tu-whoo, tu-wit, tu-whoo - a merry note.*

They are Cookham's night-time sentinels, a neighbourhood watch-keeper *par excellence* with a heritage going much further back than our own.

At the other end of the size scale, and much more likely to be seen in our Cookham gardens is the aforementioned Wren. And what delight awaits the patient observer as this most expressive little sprite takes the stage, often unexpectedly, into our private domain. On some occasions, the entrance is secret in fashion, from some dark corner, emerging but slowly from the dungeons of a low-hanging bush. Tempting glimpses of jerky movements through the undergrowth may be all that is granted initially as the wary bird weighs up the scene. Is that a cat behind the bin? Is that one of those huge globes the small humans play with coming my way? Are there any hawks about? Just as we are sure to get a full view, back into the dense foliage it goes. Then, confidence gaining, our quarry might shimmy up one of the middle twigs and gradually work its way into sight. On another occasion, it simply hurtles onto the most prominent perch without ceremony as if beamed up from some remote planet, its clamorous call filling the air as it bursts into sight. Oh, and what a sight it is! For such a tiny soul, its plumage is a miscellany of browns and buffs, tinged with greys and lighter hues, all agreeably intertwined as only a skilful designer could achieve. A notable white stripe directs our attention to the beady black eye aligned with the top of the daintiest piece of dining cutlery to be seen anywhere, perfectly crafted to deal with the smallest of reluctant meals. Seemingly under-sized wings whirr invisibly in transport whilst the faintly barred tail is hardly a tail to tell of; in fact, such as it is will normally be sported upright anyway as if stowed away until needed.

The combined effect is one of barred belly, beak and bottom in perfect harmony, never still, always alert and a presence that defies its dimensions. Whilst a comely specimen, it can be fiercely possessive, seeing off other species as well as it's own with an undaunted spirit and a sharp tongue.

Once having secured the perimeter of your garden, regular patrols are carried out, interrupted only by occasional sortie to a private saluting post. Despite its haughty nature, the Wren, it seems, is content to view life from a lowly perspective, rarely flying or perching higher than a garage roof or high fence. From this unpretentious stratum the bird makes a life-time study of the underneath of many of the things that we look down upon. Many Wrens might not know what a roof looks like from above or what Cookham looks like to a BA pilot, as they are mainly sedentary creatures unaccustomed to flights of any distance. On the other hand, they are probably far more expert at discerning a Song Thrush belly from the Mistle Thrush's than we are and can readily spot the aphids and bugs that congregate on the underside of branches to avoid the weather.

About three to six inches above ground level seems to be the standard operating altitude, dashing from cover to cover using terrain-following radar to avoid everything in between. At each landing station, the surroundings are swiftly surveyed with rapid side-to-side movements of the head, often followed by a shriek and a churr as if to signal the 'all clear'. I suspect that periscopes are employed too as I am often scalded in woodland by several that are totally unseen and could only have detected my approach by such a device. When in family mode, a pair of Wrens will be protecting 6 or more tiny white eggs in a moss-lined nest built into a crack or hole in a tree or a wall.

*Wrens*

Perhaps two, or even three clutches may be attempted in a season and good weather should ensure all fledge safely. It is however the gauntlet of their first winter that sifts the sturdy from the weak but as long as the parents produce one mature pair during their four or five year life span, the Wren population will remain stable. I have noted that, outside the breeding season, Wrens will be present in our garden for a few days, only then not to be seen for a week or more before re-appearing for short spell. Clearly they move around the neighbourhood, constantly looking for new sources of food and then repeating the circuit later. Nonetheless, there are potentially more Wrens in our domestic environment than we imagine, and I do hope your garden will be regarded as a larder by at least one of them.

There is another feature of our garden birds that may not be generally appreciated. There are two types of young produced by bird species (and I do not mean male and female!). One form of hatchling is born covered in down and with full eye-sight, able to flee the nest within twenty four hours of exiting the egg shell. These are known as nidifugous types and include ducks and waterfowl, waders and other gamefowl. Garden birds however produce young that are naked, blind and totally defenceless, taking perhaps two weeks before becoming able and interested in leaving the safety of their nest. These are known as nidicolous types and include birds of prey and garden birds. Of course, the former types gain advantage in that the young can be led to a food source and will feed for themselves whilst the nestling variety place heavy burdens on adult energies in hundreds of daily visits to the nest with food parcels. On the other hand, nidifugous young are at the mercy of the elements and predators at a much earlier stage than their nest-hidden cousins but should nestlings lose one or both parents for any reason, they are likely to perish whereas free-running young can at least fend for themselves. Whatever the pluses and minuses of these contrasting means of being launched into life on earth, both are imbued with providence.

Another birdwatching friend who lives in the Rise is Martin Britnell. Born in Maidenhead in 1959, Martin became hooked on ornithology at the young age of twelve. Encouraged by parents Cyril and Lorna, Martin teamed up with Steve Bunce and David Gibbs to study the natural history of the area between Pinkneys Green and Cookham. After twenty five years observing the mammals and birds of the area, he has noted the slow but sure decline of Sand Lizards, Badgers and Newts. Redshanks no longer breed on the marsh and Yellowhammers are far fewer than just a decade ago. Turtle Doves have become harder to find and he no longer expects to see Woodcock on Cookham Dean Common. Having worked on Mr Copas' farm for some time, Martin was one of the first to notice how much Yellowhammers and Corn Buntings seemed to be struggling to maintain their numbers. It is still possible to find small groups of Yellowhammers most years but Corn Buntings can be counted on the fingers of one hand most summers. However, the farm supplied Martin's 'Most Memorable Birding Moment' when a Black Redstart paid a visit to Long Lane. A resplendent male, cloaked in black apart from a brilliant flash of red along the ever-active tail, this was indeed a royal visit by a majestic bird. There had been high hopes that this beautiful relative of the Robin would colonise our area some twenty years ago, but alas this did not happen. And during that same period of time yet another species has dwindled into insignificance. Nightingales were once abundant in the Cookhams and the surrounding area and as recently as 1985 the Berks Bucks & Oxon Naturalists Trust described the bird as 'showing no decline'. It was as much the Nightingale as any other creature that regularly coaxed W H Hudson away from London and out to Cookham a century ago when he would regularly encounter a dozen singing in the Dean. Now we can only imagine what such a cacophony of sound that would have been.

Now it's time to move on to another part of the village.

*The High Street – 1996*

OCTOBER
    Watery sunshine, dampness and mist
    Puts up a shield against winters fist.
    The golden umbrella o'er every Cookham lane,
    A rustic be-jewelment in her regal train.

       Redwings return to bid warblers farewell,
       Spotted Flycatchers departed as well.
       Gulls follow the Thames every dusk and each dawn,
       And Skylarks once more welcome the morn.

# GOO AND GOLF

A FURTHER SECTION OF THE GREENWAY, between Cockmarsh and Cookham Moor, passes through Marsh Meadow, alongside the golf course and takes in the local sewage treatment works. This delightful walk offers some interesting sights, and smells! A resident of this stretch is another owl, the Little Owl, two or three pairs possibly being encountered with luck. I have heard as many as five adults calling to each other along here. This nine-inch (or 22.84992 cm for those preferring the current fashion) long owl is a cryptically-patterned ball of grey-brown feathers, extensively barred and mottled. With short rounded wings, and an inquisitive nature, it is as likely to be seen as much during the daytime as at night. Equipped with large and alert, yellow-rimmed eyes, they will invariably see you before you see them but prefer not to reveal their presence by flying off if they can avoid it, so it is possible to walk right underneath one and not know it. On occasions, however, if you happen to get too close for the owl's comfort, it will depart the perch in an undulating flight, dropping down several feet and then swooping up to a branch at the original height in the next tree along. Little Owls have an uncanny ability to achieve this whilst maintaining cover between the walker and itself so as not to be seen readily even in flight, but it still affords the best opportunity to see them. They tend to prefer perches in the lower half of a tree, usually with a fairly open prospect to facilitate good views of what is happening around them, being rather nosy by nature.

This dapper bird is, once again, not an indigenous species to our isles. In fact it was introduced artificially into the country and has only become established in the last one hundred years, first breeding in Northamptonshire. Unlike the Tawny Owl which is, in the main, a woodland bird, Little Owls prefer open farmland and parks, and are happy to occupy tree lines and hedgerows, especially if there is a little water around. Hunting mainly for small rodents and insects, they will work their way along the Willow Trees aside the ditch that runs from Cockmarsh. They seem to delight in playing hide and seek with the many walkers along this route, knowing it will take a purposeful observer to even catch a glimpse of them. When disturbed, the owl will bob up and down excitedly and may well begin its alarm call should young birds be in the vicinity. It is also not uncommon to see them on the ground foraging for worms and insects.

Perhaps it is in winter that the Little Owl impresses his character upon the surrounding countryside, often spotted on an exposed branch or fence-post, stoically braving a cruel frost or driving snow. Even on the bleakest of mid-winter afternoons, just before dusk, an unseen Little Owl will commence its territorial call, *kow kow*. In an instant, a response will come from the bird holding the adjacent principality, then, further off, a fainter replication, like an echo, from a third. Within a few seconds, several may be screeching their macho ownership messages to each other, broadcasting to all and sundry that 'this patch is taken'. Then, as quickly as it all started, it is ended. Messages received and understood.

*Silent rawness, numbing the ears*
*Wind in the watchers, running with tears*
*"Kow, Kow. Come Here if you dare"*
*"Kow, Kow. I won't if you stay there"*
*"Kow, Kow. You'd both best keep out"*
*"Kow, Kow. That's three more about."*
*Ah, good. I'm not alone*
*Feathered companions, all my way home.*

It's always worth being a nosy-parker at the sewage treatment works. Pongs mean insects, and insects means birds! In summer, the most numerous species will be the Sand Martins and Swallows that sweep over the site, with excited giggles, scooping up huge numbers of midges and the like. They will be joined by clouds of Starlings, bullying their way around the edges of the treatment bowls. Popping in

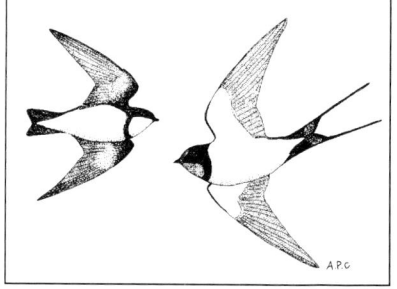
*Sand Martin & Swallow*

and out of view at the bases of the concrete structures, Robins, Dunnocks and Meadow Pipits forage nervously. Family parties of Pied Wagtails may be seen and, just possibly, the striking Yellow Wagtail might call in, especially in spring or autumn. As mentioned, I have counted over one hundred of these dazzling sulphur bobbins on one occasion, but in the main, they tend to simply utilise Cookham as an airway service centre. However, there is a spectacular wagtail that one might come across and that's the Grey Wagtail.

The male of this species is a splendid magisterial character, cloaked in elegant grey with a white eyestripe beneath his wig, and a delicate white moustache. With his hands folded behind his back, his gloved fingers are picked out in white edging and the tail to his top-coat is every bit as long as the rest of his body. A distinguished black bib contrasts with bright lemon underparts, the whole assemblage supported on long sturdy legs and spindly toes. Grey Wags are usually seen singly, always near water, flitting from one bank to another, revealing white outer tail feathers on each trip. With precise movements, tiny insects are plucked from foliage or even from the surface of moving water, weirs being one of their favourite bistros. When the much larger May Flies are about, the bird becomes quite acrobatic in pursuit of these meaty morsels. Throughout, the exceptionally long tail is constantly flicked and bobbed, just like a pole vaulter sizing up the next leap.

   A family party may well attend the open air restaurant of the Treatment Works for their regular picnic. Mrs Grey Wag and her offspring lack papa's black bib, having in its stead a dullish white chin and they busy themselves at the table under the ever-watchful gaze of their proud father. In a flurry of jerking tail feathers, several hundred insects may well be harvested by a single family party of perhaps six or seven birds in one meal-time. When the magic roundabout machines are working, spinning their four watering arms around the circular tanks, Starlings and Sparrows will be seen leaping over each arm as it approaches them as if hurdling on the spot, but the family Wagtail has learned to simply walk between the streams of water and let the arms pass overhead without undue concern. Once sated, the family group depart in the direction of the river. The treatment works are due for de-commissioning soon so we may lose some of these experiences in the years to come.

   The little stream from Cockmarsh not only hosts bank voles, fry and taddies but is a favourite feeding and drinking place for birds. Wrens, Robins, Chaffinches and Dunnocks can be regularly found whilst Chiffchaff and Blackcaps search among the lowest branches over the water in summer. One bird that occasionally uses the stream during passage time in spring and autumn is the Whinchat. A Robin-like bird in stature and behaviour, this striking traveller can be seen on watch-posts alongside the brook flicking its tail excitedly, allowing a certain proximity prior to flitting off to another position further ahead of the fortunate observer. The male is a confluence of dark and light browns on his back, a black face patch, highlighted by a white eye-stripe and a chest and belly delicately brushed in a deep-boiled toffee colour. The hen bird is similar, but generally lighter in tone. Both have a white stripe on the wing. It is our loss that such a beauty will not be seen in winter as its colouration, etched against a snowy or frosty background, would be a sight to behold.

How strange too that its very close relative, the Stonechat, is content to hold a residents permit whereas our 'Whinney' prefers passport freedom to continents far away. Twice a year these few grams of muscle and feather will traverse many of the places that most of us can only dream of visiting in our lifetime. Moving from its favoured breeding grounds in the featureless open spaces of Britain's upland areas, southern England quickly gives way to the Channel and the developed regions of Europe disappear beneath their thrashing wings as they move inexorably onto the Old World. Mediterranean climes through Spain and Morocco drive Whinney towards the dreaded dry Sahara nations of Algeria, Mali, Niger and Chad, which need be crossed before a rendezvous is possible with millions of peers along the western reaches of Africa. Studies of Whinchat and Stonechat populations have shown that the resident Stonechat has to produce twice as many young to maintain their numbers compared to the globe-trotting Whinchat, indicating that even these perilous journeys may be less hazardous for first-year younglings than trying to survive our moody winters. It must work as it has been estimated that some four thousand million birds of all types descend on Africa each autumn!

To think, a three-year old Whinchat, sitting on a Cookham fence-post, will have travelled the equivalent of the world's circumference, and still not a feather out of place.

The stream, the footpath and the railway line convene near the thirteenth tee where a busy little copse resides. A mixture of coniferous and deciduous trees ensures a number of species of a welcome in this corner of the links. The regular thwack of metal on plastic-covered rubber bands harmonises with the tweets, chacks and churrs which emanate from the copse, demanding a sojourn on the convenient bench to see what might be found. The winter picture will be one of packs of thrushes, hordes of finches, groups of Siskin and raiding parties of Long-tailed Tits, whereas summertime embraces Blackcaps, Garden Warblers and hovering Goldcrests. Great Spotted Woodpeckers busy themselves amongst the upper branches, but a close relative, the Green Woodpecker is far more likely to be seen on the golf course itself.

The Green 'Pecker is not only our largest 'woodie' but is arguably the most noticeable, not least because of its obvious bright green plumage but also by virtue of its comical but piercing call. Usually uttered in flight, this pointed parrot-like creation yelps and 'yaffles' its way from cover to cover, a brilliant yellow rump often all that is seen as one spins in the direction of the shriek. Closer up, a streaked red crown will be noted contrasting with a drooping black moustache, looking more peculiar on the female than on her handsome hubby who tints his with red to match his coronet. Its entertaining nature and strange calls have resulted in variety of nick-names such as 'Heffold Ickle', 'Yockle', 'Popinjay' and even 'Etwall'. Whilst very much at home in woodland habitat, and nesting in tree cavities, Green Woodpeckers are regularly located in open country searching for worms and insects on the ground. They can be seen well on the unencumbered and 'tidy' environs of the golf course, sometimes as a family party picnicking together.

More bizarre behaviour ensues when the bird gets an itch for a bath. Parasites congregate at the base of birds feathers and a favoured solution is to bathe in ants. With wings spread out, the bird lowers itself onto an ants nest and allows the army of defenders to squirt copious quantities of formic acid into its plumage, thereby dealing a death blow to the unwelcome guests in its down. So pleasurable does this procedure appear to be to the recipient, a state of moribundity seems to rest upon the bird, who sits with a silly grin on his face throughout. I once observed a cat stalking a Yaffle who was completely engrossed in his 'downicure'. The feline fiend, approaching from behind and supposedly unseen, gained from some 100 feet to within less than one yard before the mesmerised bird revealed its full awareness of the menace by turning swiftly on the spot and pointing its fearsome bill threateningly at the cat's nose. With an arched back, and raised fur, the predator suddenly became totally insecure in the stand-off, reversing slowly to a few yards before turning tail and scampering away with pride greatly dented. The Green Woodpecker promptly lowered itself once again onto its ants nest to complete its bath.

During this century, Green Woodpeckers have extended their range further and further north, eventually breeding in Scotland since 1951 but, as mentioned before, none have ventured over to Ireland as yet. Yaffles are most noisy during the breeding season but as this is a fairly protracted period, commencing in March, there are ample opportunities to hear one. This is just as well because, unlike it's spotted brethren, Greenies hardly drum at all and would otherwise go undetected in spring. Unfortunately, one woodpecker will almost certainly go undetected these days for the simple reason that there are none around to be detected. This is the Wryneck. This peculiar speckled brown pecker was never particularly widespread but there was a stable number of breeding pairs in the parks and woodlands of Victorian England and, up until the 1950's, several would be found in the orchards of Cookham. The aforementioned Mr E Giles recorded them nesting in the village in 1936, and no fewer than 5 pairs breeding in 1937 and one pair nesting adjacent to Lesser Spotted Peckers in the Dean in 1942. However, in post-war years, with many woodlands decimated for the war effort, and numerous orchards untended for similar reasons, records diminished and now a Wryneck in Cookham would be a very rare sight, which is a shame because, apart from any other reason, I haven't seen one at all yet!

One species regularly encountered on this walk, however, is the Goldfinch. Once known as the seven-coloured linnet, and a favourite cage bird of Victoriana, birdcatchers would travel out from London to Cockmarsh to net as many as they could. Cockney trappers didn't care too much what else fell unwittingly into their clutches. Even

*Goldfinch*

Sparrows would earn them 2d each whilst Yellowhammers and Greenfinches would fetch 3d. Linnets raised a handsome 8d to 10d each but the prize of each safari would be the Goldfinches which would sell for 18d each (7½p in current coinage, but worth only 1½p in its time). Young birds were favourite in summer as they continue to sing into the autumn months whereas adults tend to be less vociferous until the following spring. This dainty member of the creation is indeed a thing of beauty to behold. A veritable feathered harlequin, its silvery bill protrudes through a red face mask, surrounded in white cheeks, whilst a black crown and collar contrasts with a warm brown back and a buff and russet chest.

The wings are black, edged with white and emblazoned with distinctive yellow bands. Beyond its brilliant white rump, the bird is completed by a deeply notched tail of black. A perky bird, the Goldfinch, and very much a favourite through the ages, named Gold Spink, or Gowd Spink, Jack

Nicker, King Harry and Red Cap. More appropriate to my mind was Proud Tailor, which so much befits its manner of displaying its adornments in catwalk fashion, and Thistle Finch, a name describing well one of the Goldfinches preferred habitats. Family parties will descend upon an outcrop of thistles, busily chirruping their way through the maze using their petite bills to search out the tiniest insects who thought they were safe tucked well down in the deepest crevices of the thistle head, or more particularly, the seeds themselves.

There is something soothing about an encounter with a Charm of Goldfinches on a hot summers day, with their warm high-pitched *sweeits* and *twitits* spread like butter on the air, accompanied by the buzzing of blue-bottles and the rattles of the thistles themselves. The seeds are surgically removed and detached from their little feathery parachutes which fly off in the breeze to form their own flocks. Their colouration picked out against the purple thistle backdrop, all the birds seem to talk at once, especially when it comes time to relocate when all of them seem to call *lesgo, lesgo* simultaneously. In winter, large numbers gather together on waste and open land, maybe as many as one hundred being seen, actively scanning hedgerows and field margins for food. Teamwork is important for many species of small birds in winter, many pairs of eyes making less work in finding scarce fodder and also in keeping watch for Sparrowhawks whilst they are more exposed with less foliage around. It is fortunate that our regal Jack has survived near extinction at the hands of Victorian cage mongers. The slopes of Winter Hill and the open ground of Marsh Meadow are two areas where one might expect to experience the delights of this noble finch.

*Beauty in kaleidoscope,*
*Bringing with it summer's hope,*
*Bright enough to never mope,*
*King Harry is the name.*

At the northern end of Marsh Meadow, Farmer Copas and the children of Herries and Holy Trinity Schools have combined to create a small pond and wildlife area. With water of different depths, a small island and a range of suitable plants, an interesting habitat is forming. Many birds visit the pool to drink and Mallard Ducks have already viewed it in the prospect of a new home. In time, and with minimum disturbance, passing waders might call at the shallow end to inspect the muddy rim of this new piece of habitat.

Yet another spectacle is given at this location, essentially in the autumn and winter evenings. As the dusk returns from its secret daytime hiding place, the air begins to sparkle with white images flecked against a darkening sky. Firstly, just a few might be seen, then small groups and finally, as darkness ensues, great aerial rafts of them go streaming over. These are our county gulls. Having foraged and preened their way through the daylight hours, each in their turn commence the evening journey to their chosen roosting site. For many, this will be one of the west London reservoirs where up to ten thousand may gather on each expanse of water. It is worth a mid-winter visit to one of them just to experience the exuberant arrival of vast numbers of birds as a blizzard of silvery forms rain down in front of looming black storm clouds. But locally, those gulls which have spent their day in fields and meadows abutting the river, work their way along the Thames Valley, and then the M4 motorway.

Over Cookham, huge numbers wend their way silently in v-formation groups, the differing sizes of Herring Gulls and Lesser Black-backed Gulls with the smaller Black-headed and Common Gull being quite obvious. This regulated air display may last up to one hour, with birds probably coming from as far as south Oxford, the lower ones standing out against the darkening green slopes of Cliveden, the higher ones silhouetted against a kaleidoscopic evening sky. This scene signifies to the observer the comforting confirmation of another day successfully completed, as timely as church-bell chimes. For the gulls themselves, it represents a victorious home-coming flight following the survival of another winters day during which it is essential to find sufficient energy-giving food to enable each bird to see the cold night through on their exposed watery roost. Although this proves safer for the majority compared to roosting in fields with foxes to contend with, each night there will be those that succumb to the conditions, to be washed up on the reservoir banks next morning with no epitaph to record their adventures and exploits. Those that join us from afar may have discovered where daylight comes from to spread itself to the ends of the earth, seen many a dawn robed in red, found the balances that support the clouds and the doors that give the sea its bounds, but keep all these things to themselves. Birds of habit, providing us with a daily dose of mystery.

One who greatly appreciates this regular spectacle from his village garden is Peter Gaines. Peter moved to Cookham from South Wales in 1958 to take up a teaching post nearby. He met his wife-to-be, Irene, who had lived in the village since 1950 whilst working for Commander Giddy. Quiet village life, and the enthusiasm of stepson and local birdwatcher, Alan Chapman, brought Peter to the fascination of the avian scene around him and an introduction to what was to become an ongoing hobby and interest.

Peter and Irene's earliest recollections of local birdlife include the amazing scenes of the 62/63 winter, one of the harshest in living memory, and which conspired to position waterfowl such as Coot and Moorhen in their School Lane garden as floodwaters bathed much of the village for some days. An unexpected visitor to the Gaines' residence one year was George the injured Tawny Owl, which Peter and Irene nursed back to health, a close-encounter experience determining that a re-name to Georgina was appropriate! This service to bird-kind became habitual with up to 28 residents in the garden bird hospital in one particular year.

The Gaines' remember what might have been the last Rookery in Cookham, further along School Lane. They also recall Dr Richards, from the Dean, collecting any young Rooks dislodged from their nests and eventually releasing them into Regents Park where he was attempting to re-establish a long-lost Rookery. Unfortunately the London Crows made sure his attempts were fruitless.

So, the Rise fully explored, where might we seek out next?

---

NOVEMBER
Fog abounding, rain resounding
When will the sun shine again?
But Cookham is nestling
In the arms of the mist
Whilst humming autumnal refrain.

    A myriad Starling tumble down on the lea
    Midst the Lapwing and Black-headed Gulls.
    Blackbirds put song into hearts numbed by cold,
    And the Storm Cock serenades Highland Bulls.

# THERE'S AN OLD MILL BY THE STREAM

WELL, THERE USED TO BE! Halfway along Mill Lane, the stream comes swinging in from the northern side and sprints off towards the River at the far end of the footpath, anxious to thrust itself into the murky, swirling depths of Old Father Thames, and frantic to hear all the gossip since it last departed it's bigger brother at Cookham Bridge. Entrapped within the loop formed by the stream are the grounds of Odney and Formosa, a tranquil corner fashioned from formal gardens, a cricket pitch, mature trees and a leafy lane. Under the watchful eye of a magnificent Weeping Beech, the island birds frolic amongst lush trees, mown lawns and a tube of scrub surrounding the river-bound footpath.

The birdlife of Formosa was better recorded last century than of late with an active gamekeeper, one Mr Briggs, keen to add any unusual species to the ever-expanding collection of Mrs De Vitre, wife of Reverend George, curate of the Dean. Tree Sparrow, Hawfinches, Lesser Spotted Peckers, Water Rail, Hobby, Nightjar, and Merlin were all obtained by this worthy. Aided by Mr Goddon, the Cookham Ferryman, Short-eared Owl, Scoter, Tufted Duck, Goosander, Slavonian Grebe, Red-throated Diver, and Quail were also added to the good lady De Vitre's immobile flock. With the help of a certain Mr Brown of Cookham Dean, other species such as Ringed Plover, Green Sandpiper, Common Tern, Lesser Tern, Black Tern, Golden Eagle, Osprey, Buzzard, and Great Grey Shrike were soon on static display. Mr Briggs blasted Bramblings, Snow Bunting, Cirl Bunting, and Hoopoe alike. Mr John Ford, taxidermist of Cookham was also kept busy with Little Bittern, Bittern, Great Snipe, Knot, Greylag Goose, Velvet Scoter, Mandarin, and Cormorant. Mr Gould, a lock-keeper of his day, upon finding an extremely rare Grey Phalarope on the Thames "struck it with his oar, but the bird, though much exhausted, managed to escape". Small wonder then, that in our more enlightened times, few of these species grace this particular corner of heaven's aviary.

Many of these records are courtesy of Dr Richard Bowdler Sharpe. Born in London on 22nd November 1847, Dr Sharpe became an ornithologist in his teens whilst living with his parents, Thomas and Elizabeth Sharpe in Holly Lodge, Hills Lane, Cookham. In those days, he met Emily Burrows, daughter of James Burrows, the Cookham shoe magnate. Emily was born in 1843 when her father was just 16, and they lived at The Elms, with his mother and a number of lodgers and servants. She married Sharpe in 1867 and it was at this time that he was recording the bird life (and death) in the village. He too established a collection of stuffed specimens though there is no record of what it contained. Almost anyone of substance in those days probably had a collection. The unfortunate inmates of this after-life imprisonment are doubtless gathering dust in some museum loft or basement, if indeed they have survived even to that. On a national scale, Victorian England must have been responsible for the wholesale slaughter of millions of our most beautiful birds. Against this history, it is hardly surprising that the French and Italians today cock a snook at our feeble appeals to them to leave 'our' birds alone as they trap and shoot anything flying in our direction each spring!

However, Bowdler-Sharpe went on to atone for this in some way when, in his later years, he became the first librarian to the Zoological Society in London and managed to catalogue the *History of the Birds of Europe*, also being responsible for 27 volumes of the British Museum's Catalogue of Bird Skins in the 1890's. In the summer of 1996, some months after researching the history of this notable birder, I was offered the opportunity to visit the British Ornithological Union's museum in Tring, Hertfordshire. The origins of the museum stemmed from being constructed as a 21st birthday present for Walter Rothschild. In his later years, having amassed the largest collection of stuffed birds in the known world, Lord Walter was obliged to sell it all to the USA at a time of financial exigency. Subsequently, the London Natural History Museum moved many of the nation's bird's skins to this research facility which has now grown, re-establishing its reputation globally. Visitors come from all over the world to study at the centre, learning about plumage differences of birds from various regions, and creating the paintings that fill the pages of modern field guides and conservation study material. I was being shown just a handful of the one million skins of dead birds, many dating back to Victorian times, when I happened to notice one of the specimens bore a label filled out by no less a person than R B Sharpe! This was a Chiffchaff shot or found dead in Cookham in 1871. It transpired that this was just one of the many thousands of specimens identified and catalogued by the indefatigable Sharpe one hundred years ago, which constituted a somewhat 'spooky' experience!

Nowadays, as the Thames surges past Formosa, it might wash the underneath of a lazy Mallard or two, or perhaps lap up against the sides of a pair of Mandarin but few of the feathered wonders which graced the sights of Biggs' gun can be anticipated. However, some avian enjoyment is still to be had at the expense of the young Coots and Moorhen when they begin to venture away from the bankside. Until they become accustomed to the rate of flow of this watery conveyor belt, they can soon be taken several yards down-stream whilst mama's eyes are diverted and the frantic effort they have to expend to get back to her can look quite comical. Even without wings, they seem to almost quit the water as their tiny legs thrash the surface and they reach amazing speeds on tip-toes.

   There have been occasional rarities nearby in recent times, the most remarkable perhaps being the juvenile Shag which appeared in May 1993, taking up residence at Boulters Lock, but regarding the stretch of river down to Cookham Bridge as part of its territory. It stayed for nearly three years, becoming quite confiding and allowing observers to monitor it obtaining iridescent dark green adult plumage over that period of time. On one occasion, locating it on Ray Mill Island, I was able to approach it inch by inch, over a ten minute period, until my foot was within 12 inches of the bird. Throughout, it studied my every move but, by keeping my gaze mainly away from the bird, it seemed to assume, correctly, that I meant it no harm and allowed this amazing proximity. Needless to say, I had no camera with me to photograph its dainty head, long hooked bill and incredible bottle-green eyes! After enjoying each others company for some ten further minutes, someone else arrived fifty yards away and the bird took to the water. The incident stirred a recollection of a trip to Norfolk with my friend Martin Gostling and my son Mark on which occasion we found a Shag injured in a field. Between us we were able to pick up the bird and form a human chain to pass it to the one nearest the water who waded out and placed it safely in the sea where at once it revived and moved off. In the hand, they are much smaller than I had imagined. Unfortunately, the Boulters Lock bird was found dead in February 1996.

   The Thames of course has been the stage for a regular bird spectacle – the annual Swan Upping. Since the 12th century, the Mute Swan has been afforded a privileged position under the protection of the Monarchy. Every year, in July, the 'Royal Swan Master' as he was titled, would proceed down the Thames to catch and mark every cygnet hatched in the previous season. Special permission was extended to the City of London Livery Companies during the 15th century to also be involved in the process and a scheme of different marking for each group has evolved. The Vintners and Dyers are the sole remaining Livery companies following the tradition. Each summer, a small flotilla of boats, suitably bedecked with corporate and regal banners, makes its colourful way along the river in search of these elegant fowl. The three crews agree amicably as to which swans receive which identification as the monarch owns half and the Livery companies one quarter each. The Queen's birds have no mark, the Dyer's a mark on one side and the Vintner's one mark each side. The process has its roots in ownership of birds for the table, up to twelve birds facilitating the annual Swan Feast held by the companies until recent times. However, in a more enlightened age, the Swan Study Group from Oxford University accompany the Uppers, checking health and statistics of the captured birds and comparing the figures with previous records, and the event has become more ceremonial with interests in conservation and the well-being of the birds themselves.

Mind you, I wonder if the swans themselves see it that way. Harried and harassed from all sides, an unsuspecting bird suddenly finds itself surrounded by burly blokes leaning perilously out of their tiny vessels attempting to get a firm grip of the reluctant bird. With much hissing and wing-flapping, each quarry is eventually cornered and hauled unceremoniously out of the water to be checked. Let it be known that a full-sized Mute Swan on its own territory can be a mean defender of its environment and itself! It takes a brave person indeed to purposefully attempt to capture one as I learned when confronted by one on the M4 motorway on one occasion. Having apparently collided with an overhead power line, the confused

*Swan & Cygnets*

creature was wandering all over the road conspiring to being a danger to itself and everyone else. By chance, I discovered that throwing a blanket over its head had the immediate effect of causing the bird to go straight down on the ground with its head curled up on its back. Perhaps I could introduce this technique to the Queen's trappers? But no doubt, over the centuries, there will have been many a tale to tell of bedraggled 'Uppers' being rescued from the clutches of a grand-daddy swan or the clamouring waters of Old Father Thames!

Under the reign of Elizabeth I, hundreds of different markings would have been necessary to affirm ownership, but in this day of Elizabeth II, the annual pageant is a much more local affair with simplified markings applied. In that bygone age, the entire nation's waterways were covered by Deputy Swan Masters, reporting to the 'Master of the King's Game of Swans' who was a Gentleman of the Court responsible for the royal table. Cookham has been privileged to be the home of two recent Swan Masters. A notable character is John Turk who was born in 1913 and raised at the family home, Rivergate, which nestles in between the River, The Ferry Inn and the historic twelfth-century Holy Trinity church. His father Fred was a third-generation boat builder and waterman and moved to Cookham from Kingston to run a couple of boathouses bought by John's grandfather. Fred and his wife Muriel came to Rivergate in 1913, but it was not until 1954 that John returned from duty with the Merchant Navy and the Thames Conservancy to take over the business due to his father's ill health. The bustling boatyard gave birth to a steady stream of skiffs, launches and electric vessels. A charging yard was constructed where the electric powered boats could have their appetites sated overnight, sufficient for twenty or thirty miles journeying the next day. The river scene then was much calmer, albeit being a well-used waterway. Paddles, punt poles, puffing chimneys and purring electric engines gave but a subtle backdrop to busy-ness compared to overpowered outboards, odorous oils and ocean-going noise machines that ply the father of rivers today.

It was during the time he served with the Conservancy in Oxford that John met his wife Marjorie, who had moved there from her birth-place Muswell Hill, via a sojourn of some years at Westcliffe on Sea. Marjorie's family name was Nixon and in fact, her brother was the celebrated television magician David Nixon who fascinated young and old with his warm sonality and conjuring skills. Many of Cookham's ladies will remember when, in their youth, Marjorie took over from Mrs Chapel as Brown Owl to the First Cookham Brownie group, eventually forming a second group as numbers grew. John remembers well the regattas on the river in the 1920's. There used to be two each year. In mid-summer, the Amateur

Regatta took place whilst the Rag Regatta was held in September. One popular event was the Nippy Race involving a fit young man as a canoe paddler and a young lady standing in the prow with a tray full of cups and saucers trying hard not to be dislodged. Up to a dozen teams competed in the race and the crockery was always supplied by Joe Lyons. Tilting with mop-ended poles was another favourite, a forerunner of *Gladiators* it seems.

As Inspector of Navigation with the Thames Conservancy since 1948, John possessed all the credentials to be appointed Royal Swan Master following a family tradition going back to his uncle Richard who was Royal Waterman and Swan Marker to the Worshipful Company of Vintners in 1901. John's father Fred then became the Swan Keeper on July 1st, 1922 until John took over on July 1st 1963. Many of these men were also Royal Watermen whose duties included transporting the monarch to special functions such as the State Opening of Parliament. John was the first 'Up-river' Royal Waterman, a position more recently taken on by Tony Hobbs.

In a brilliant red tunic, John and his predecessors made a striking picture as they led their crews along the river keeping a beady eye open for any swans lurking in a quiet side-water or tributary. The sixty five mile procession from Sunbury to Abingdon takes place in the third week of July and is the last remaining example of the custom. The six skiffs make slow progress, stopping at local hostelries for each overnight rest. The Thames Riviera has been employed for this task, as has the White Hart in Henley but Odney was the main centre for accommodation from war-time until 1965. Over the years, the Uppers have seen the fortunes of their quarry wax and wane greatly. Staines and Windsor used to have several hundred of these magnificent creatures and the Marlow herd gradually dispersed over the years. Fewer breeding sites due to greater use of the river and more vessels moored along its banks have had a major impact but probably the greatest reaper of their numbers was the toxic angler's weights that, over many years, caused tremendous loss amongst the birds as they either swallowed them or got entangled in the tackle. Rescue Centres around the country began reporting major increases in birds being taken in for lead poisoning treatment during the seventies and eighties and the population fell dramatically. With help from the government and fishing tackle manufacturers, non-toxic equivalents were produced and fishermen were urged to change their equipment as soon as possible. This combined action served to turn around the situation and today many swan havens are beginning to see numbers restored. In part, this will have been due to careful monitoring of breeding groups by teams such as the Royal Swan Uppers who have therefore contributed to the improving status of these beautiful birds.

After 30 years of upholding this tradition, John Turk finally handed over the Master's tunic to David Barber in 1993. Of course, living and working on the river for so many years, Mr Turk's interest in the riparian birdlife extends well beyond the post-breeding week of swan upping. He recalls finding a swan's nest with thirteen eggs compared to the normal five to nine. He was also often called in to deal with a variety of swan incidents including one which brought down power cables in Bourne End but survived, and another that fell into a water treatment plant and was injured. John by now had a pen in his grounds where swans could recuperate but eventually professional services such as Save Our Swans in Windsor were established with full veterinary support.

*Bewick's Swan*

On one occasion, the police directed John to where the carcasses of seven swans laid, slaughtered by cross-bow fire. A little later, his friend John Field found some boys shooting at the swans with a cross-bow, seriously injuring one unfortunate bird. A severe telling off from the Swan Master was all that was necessary to ensure the lads never did that again. Oh that it would be sufficient for today's wayward ones! Not that all the swans John found on the river were of the Mute variety. A Bewick's Swan was found on one occasion and Black Swans were regularly found following the import of twelve pairs to Pangbourne from Australia by the Wincarnos Wine Company from Perth.

In more recent times, John has noticed the steady decline of the Little Grebe, or Dabchick, on the river. Once quite common, they have been flushed into the many tributaries by the more consistent wave action created by modern river craft. However, during the same period, the larger and even more striking Great Crested Grebe has become a regular incumbent of many a stretch of the Thames. It was indeed most rare on the river even forty or so years ago, as recounted by Robert Gibbings in his book "Sweet Thames Run Softly" in 1940. Gibbings rowed the entire length of the river in the previous year and recorded the plant and animal life he encountered. He noted his hope of spying Great Crested Grebe when he got to Shiplake near the end of his long journey, but although they were reported to be nesting there, he never saw them. Now there are pairs along the whole length of the river. Herons too have remained common and Coots have gradually taken over the mainstream breeding territories from the Moorhen which, like the Dabchick, have been obliged to retire to the side-waters. However, as the Swans re-establish their numbers, let us hope the annual Swan Upping ceremony continues.

*Little Grebe*

# ODNEY AND THE VILLAGE

MANY AN ODNEY VISITOR will have witnessed this water-borne round-up as they took their ease in the quietude of this exclusive resting place. Strolling through the formal gardens, or contemplating the lily pads on the pool, they will be surrounded by many other birds that the majority never notice. Treecreepers secretly encircle great boles a few feet away from a sleepy intern. Nuthatches on covert operations tap at any potential food safe. Kingfishers swoop low over the tennis courts obliged by the oblivion of pretending Wimbledon champions. Wagtails hop un-noticed around the feet of fishers and boaters alike and Chaffinches chase crumbs amongst the Clark's and Bally's beneath the picnic tables. Encouraged by this invisibility, Jackdaws and Magpies frolic on the lawns whilst Blackbirds and Song Thrushes become spectral diners in the path-side borders. Nor does the holiday mood deprive visitors only of their sight; their hearing fails too. The resident Robins hail each other heartily without recognition. The mighty Mistle Thrush cries out with gusto, but would only be applauded if he could replicate the dinner gong! The Magpies croak and cackle with a volume to challenge the 11am Concord, but life for the visitor goes on un-appreciatively. For the local, a summer's walk along the footpath across Odney Common to the weir will be rewarded with close encounters with Swallows which dash across the path to inspect each passer-by closely. Linnets and Goldfinches line up along the garden walls to watch the procession of fishermen, courting couples and stream-bound children. At the weir itself, Chiffchaffs and Blackcaps entertain and Grey Wagtails bob from bank to bank. A Hobby may pass through playing hide and seek with high-flying Mayfly and a Heron might 'crank' overhead.

Mill Lane too offers prospective bird-finders an opportunity to get a little closer to small birds, especially along the overgrown sector surrounding the footpath. This natural portico to the river beyond is often alive with various woodland and garden species and always promises Great Spotted Woodpecker, Treecreeper, and views of Kingfisher again on the adjacent stream.

The Odney Club itself has some history concerning birds. John Speden Lewis, founder of the Lewis Partnership in 1864, was a keen naturalist and ornithologist. When Odney was purchased by the Partnership as a country club for staff members, Mr Lewis moved a collection of owls from his London home to the club, establishing an aviary in what was known as the 'Owl Garden'. This area now houses the Partnership Management Training Centre, but for many years held this impressive collection of owls from such diverse places as New Guinea, Borneo, East Asia and Africa. There were a few sunbirds, pheasants, parrots and peacocks, but the anti-social vocal habits of the latter caused such complaint from neighbours that this section of the collection had to be disposed of. Throughout the time of the developing collection at Odney, John Lewis appointed a curator for the aviaries, Miss E Chawner, a member of the Avicultural Society and a writer for their Journal. She lived at the club from 1927, adding her own species to the collection until, eventually, Lewis repaired to the Leckford Estate in 1932. Some of the birds, and Miss Chawner's own expertise, were transported to Hampshire but many of the owls were disposed of by auction at that time. The list below replicates the details of the public auction.

| | | | | |
|---|---|---|---|---|
| 1 Barred Wood Owl | £8 | 3 Tawny Owls | £1 1s 6d |
| 1 Ural Owl (would breed) | £5 | 2 Woodford's Owls (believed pr) | £16 |
| 2 Malayan Fishing Owls | £12 | 2 Malayan Fishing Owls (mated pr) | £14 |
| 2 Brown Fishing Owls | £20 | Pr Eagle Owls (reared young) | £6 |
| 3 Eagle Owls (young) | £4 10s | Pr Eagle Owls (have laid) | £25 |
| 1 Bengal Eagle Owl | £5 | 2 Spotted Eagle Owls (mated, laid) | £6 |
| 1 Grey Eagle Owl | £3 | 2 Grey Eagle Owls (mated, bred) | £6 |
| 1 Savigny's Eagle Owl | £8 | 2 Milky Eagle Owls (mated pair) | £30 |
| 3 Virginia Eagle Owl | £6 30s | 2 Virginia Eagle Owls (young) | £10 |
| 2 Magellan's Eagle Owls | £6 | 1 Magellan's Eagle Owl (young) | £3 |
| 1 Snowy Owl | £8 | 2 Snowy Owls (pair, hen injured) | £12 12s |
| Pr Spectacled Owls | £12 | 3 Spectacled Owls | £18 |
| 2 Scops Owls | £6 | 2 Plume Footed Scops (nested) | £5 |
| 2 Plume Footed Scops | £5 | 1 Plume Footed Scops (breeder) | £2 10s |
| 2 Burmese Scops | £4 | 2 Malayan Scops | £5 |
| 3 White Faced Scops | £12 | 3 Ceram Scops | £4 |
| 1 Sth American Scops | £5 | 2 Tengmalm's Owls (have laid) | £10 |
| 2 Red Sea Little Owls | £8 | 2 Hutton's Little Owls (have laid) | £10 |
| 2 Chile Burrowing Owls | £5 | 6 Peruvian Burrowing Owls | £15 |
| 1 Sparrow Owl | £4 | 2 Indian Barn Owls (have hatched) | £4 |
| 1 Bay Owl | £15 | 1 English Barn Owl | 7s 6d |
| 2 Brazilian Barn Owls | £3 10s | 2 W Indian Barn Owls (have laid) | £3 |

Today, there are no Barn Owls left, only Tawny Owl may be heard near Odney, as a symbolic representation of this international convocation.

Much of the history of the Cookhams is contained within the nooks and crannies of the Village itself. Today it is the magnet which attracts tourists from all over the globe with its picturesque and time-laden street and its 'olde-worlde' buildings. Time is locked into the ageing brick walls and weathered timbers like a prison, never to be released until the last inquisitive traveller has paced the hallowed pavements from end to end. Somehow, the Village conspires to reflect centuries of antiquity despite cars parked bumper-to-bumper the clock round and incessant traffic whirling inches away from the elbows of every nation. Oblivion to anything post-past sets in like rigor mortis as tales of bygone lives seep out from doors and windows. The eyes and ears of the walls store untold biographies which fascinate even today and when we've gone back as far as recollection and records allow, there is still more that these walls could tell us.

*Barn Owl*

Older residents will recall the changes of businesses that have given the Village its life over the decades. Tucks, the bakery and the dairy, the cobblers which is now a dress shop. Then the Old Apothecary still named as such even though a private residence; W E Day, the butchers which was bought by Robert Court before he in turn moved on. Then there was another butchers, Jack Smith, who is brother-in-law to the present meat merchant in the Parade, Peter Giggs. The first Post Office was inside Stutchberry's, the grocery shop but later became its own establishment when the barbers shop closed. Stutchberry's itself became Budgens Stores. Mr Francis ran another bakery on the site of Vine Cottage and was renowned for his doughnuts. Next to the adjacent restaurant was the old farm owned by Mrs Burnap's grandparents. The old barn there was used for Guide meetings and by a family cleaners business by the Bora family from France and was also the reason Barnside Garage subsequently became so named. Next door was the International Stores and a gents hairdressers whilst opposite the blacksmiths was a shoe repair business run by lame Mr Lake who would arrive on his tricycle every day. Miss Slack owned the sweet and newspaper shop.

It's true enough that the bird-life in the Village itself might not be much to write about, much of it thriving out of sight in the pretty back gardens of the High Street dwellings. The church-yard of Holy Trinity may have been the resting place for twelve centuries of Cookhamites but it is also a haven for a variety of garden birds and summer visitors. Blackbirds sing psalms from the yew trees, occasionally accompanied by a pilgrim Chiffchaff. Swifts screech their praises around the bell tower as if trying to evangelise any bats that reside there whilst good parishioners emerge, borne on the day's inspiration, and oblivious to this ongoing chorus. I am still contemplating whether or not birds that perform in close proximity to the songs of praise of God's people and His angels do so with even greater alacrity!

> *Praise the Lord from the earth*
> *You great creatures and all ocean depths.....*
> *Wild animals and all cattle*
> *Small creatures and flying birds.....*
> *Praise the Lord.*
> *Ps 148: 7-10*

When the churchyard is quieter, Dunnocks delve around the bases of sepulchre stones whilst Robins flit between the tops of them. Despite sharing the same habitats since the creation, these two species seem not to get on well together. The Dunnock for its part would most likely prefer a quiet existence and tolerates any intrusion by turning the other cheek; but not so the Robin. I suspect this bird is secretly a hypocrite! To us he seems a close friend, revelling in and acknowledging his special place in our midst, charming us with his confiding nature, wooing us with his melodic song and striking features. However, once our back is turned, he lauds this prominence over all who would dare to threaten his status with humans. Unfortunately, the timid Dunnock is often his first target. You see, the Hedge Sparrow too would be happy to have a special place in our hearts and to dance for us and serenade us; indeed her song is perhaps even more soothing than the redbreast's. But the Dunnock is not interested in status or position and will quickly submit to her querulous peer. Whereas most species only protect its territory in the breeding season, the Robin is an all-year round defender of its domicile, taking on other types as well as its own. It is not unknown for Robins to fight to the death, the very bill through which he captivates us with his song used to fearsome results on a less able opponent.

In our country, the Robin is somewhat unique, yet it belongs to a wider family of birds with a large number of related species. Historically a bird of ancient forest glades, it quickly picked out areas cleared by man and stayed on even as houses and people occupied them. Although essentially a sedentary creature, some do migrate to northern Europe and Spain but they seem to be mainly youngsters displaced during winter territorial disputes. In the main, however, progeny will find a disused home quite close to where they were hatched, supplanting older birds which have ascended to that greater ancestral abode. Robins in adult plumage are difficult to identify individually. Some believe that male and female can be separated by the shape of the grey line above the fore-head but some variations of patterning occur anyway, and indeed, albino ones are not unusual.

*Robin*

Many folk still believe the Robin is a winter-time (or more precisely, a Christmas) visitor, overlooking their continued presence the year long. Perhaps it is the Christmas card imagery that heightens our awareness at this special time, and the sheer neighbourliness of this bird that represents the Christmas message. There is no doubt that a prominent red breast thrusting out of a snow-covered border or proudly disported from the bird-table in the otherwise bare apple tree brings a sense of warmth and anticipation of the milder months to come. So thrilled are we with the appearance of 'our' Robin in our garden, we can easily forget that each bitter winter's night is a battle for survival for each of our smaller birds. A healthy Robin would normally weigh in at around twenty grams in summer but can easily be slimmed down to fifteen as winter takes its toll. In summer, body weight loss overnight is perhaps only half a gram – easily made up with an hour or two's feeding. In winter however, the energy taken to keep warm in the cold blackness may reduce weight by as much as two grams which some individuals will find impossible to make up in snow-covered terrain. And so our feeding stations become more and more important. Please do remember to keep them topped up in harsh weather and to have un-frozen water available too. Bread, fat and meal-worms are perhaps the most valuable sources of energy to provide and this recipe will attract other species too. It will mean tolerating Starlings, of course, but once they are sated, put some more out and the other birds will follow.

Not surprisingly, Robins are amongst our more numerous species, perhaps with as many as five million individuals. At any one time the population comprises a large number of first-year young, a good percentage of two-to-five year-olds and some OAP's of around ten years. As with most small birds, probably only a quarter of them reach their first birthday, but having done so, sufficient of them will learn the secrets of survival enough to seed several broods in order to maintain overall numbers. Those that do not make the first year will have met their demise at the blunt end of a car, the sharp end of a cat or the unseen end of a window. Starvation reaps its crop every winter whilst Sparrowhawks graze on them in summer and, in the past, Cookham's Red-backed Shrikes would also have taken their toll. We also tend to forget that birds are subject to numerous parasites and diseases. Fungal infections cause feather loss and pollution of the environment is becoming a greater threat than ever before. But, for our benefit, sufficient numbers survive these harassments to grace our garden year on year.

In springtime, as the sap rises in their bones, males will be seen feeding their valentines in tender courtship, having already chosen their prospective retreat, within which a brood of five or six young will be raised, after two weeks of hatching. The fledglings often confuse the observer into thinking another species has taken to visiting the garden, as the young look nothing like their parents. Just as human sixteen year-olds like to wear *anything* that separates them from their parents, so do sixteen-day Robin youngsters, with a barred head, speckled chest and patterned upper parts. These tiny balls of enjoyment are often found wandering around the lawn in summer looking pretty pathetic and it is tempting to pick them up and take them inside for protection. However, this is rarely necessary and does not always result in success, as they need constant attention. It is preferable to place them in a safer place away from marauding cats and leave their parents to locate them by their bleatings. Only if it is known for certain that both parents have deserted them or perished in some way is it worth attempting to emulate their ministrations.

If your garden has yet to prove attractive to Robins, it may be worth erecting a suitable nest box in a quiet corner of the garden, on a wall or tree, with the entrance facing north. This entrance should not be a hole as suited to titmice, but a slot the full width of the box and about two or three inches deep. Positioned at approximately five feet from the ground, and preferable partially concealed by clematis or honeysuckle, a pair might soon show interest.

Of course, the Robin is not only cast as the star of Christmas cards, but has been the cause of much poetry in its more recent life-time, albeit without due stipend. A familiar example is:

> The north wind doth blow
> And we shall have snow
> And what will the Robin do then,
> Poor thing?
>
> He will sleep in the barn
> To keep himself warm
> And hide his head under his wing
> Poor thing.

None is perhaps more well-known than the rhyming tale of "Who killed Cock Robin". A renowned ornithologist, David Lack, researched numerous sources of the various versions of this sequel, and its earlier epic "The Marriage of Cock Robin and Jenny Wren". Whilst clearly originating hundreds of years ago, the fourteen verses which seem most definitive hail from the eighteenth century and Lack records them in *The Robin*, a book written by Chris Mead, who worked for the British Trust for Ornithology for over twenty years:

*Robin's Rest Home? The Rise Cemetery*

1 - *Who killed Cock Robin?*
*I, said the Sparrow,*
*With my bow and arrow,*
*And I killed Cock Robin.*

2 - *Who did see him die?*
*I, said the Fly,*
*With my little eye,*
*And I saw him die.*

3 - *Who catched his blood?*
*I, said the Fish,*
*With my little dish,*
*And I catched his blood.*

4 - *Who made his shroud?*
*I, said the Beetle,*
*With my little needle,*
*And I made his shroud.*

5 - *Who shall dig his grave?*
*I, says the Owl,*
*With my spade and showl,*
*And I will dig his grave.*

6 - *Who will be the parson?*
*I, says the Rook,*
*With my little book,*
*And I will be the parson.*

7 - *Who will be the clerk?*
*I, says the Lark,*
*If 'tis not in the dark,*
*And I will be the clerk*

8 - *Who'll carry him to the grave?*
*I, says the Kite,*
*If 'tis not in the night,*
*And I'll carry him to the grave.*

9 - *Who will carry the link?*
*I, says the Linnet,*
*I'll fetch it in a minute,*
*And I will carry the link.*

10 - *Who will be chief mourner?*
*I, says the Dove,*
*For I mourn for my love,*
*And I'll be the chief mourner.*

11 - *Who will bear the pall?*
*We, says the Wren,*
*Both the cock and the hen,*
*And we will bear the pall.*

12 - *Who will sing a psalm?*
*I, says the Thrush,*
*As she sat in a bush,*
*And I will sing a psalm.*

13 - *Who will toll the bell?*
*I, says the Bull,*
*Because I can pull,*
*And so Cock Robin farewell.*

14 - *All the birds of the air,*
*Fell to sighing and sobbing,*
*When they heard the bell toll,*
*For poor Cock Robin.*

The story seems to acknowledge the elitism of the Robin though one might have thought at least some of the birds would have welcomed his passing!

# Brookside

To the south of the village and constraining the ravenous ogre of urban development lies the common. This piece of land has held various names in its time and even today some confusion surrounds its proper title. In the original Lease of 1597, signed by Stafford on behalf of Queen Elizabeth, the land was known as 'Withbrook and Cookham Marsh' and was available to the parishioners for pasture and farming for a yearly rendering of "forty one shillings of lawful money of England, at the Feast of Communication of the Blessed Virgin Mary and St Michael the Archangel". It essentially takes its modern name from the brook which runs through it and since 1780, the name Widbrook applied to both land and water. However, many of the places around the common contain white in their name; White Place Farm, Whitebrook Cottage, and some modern maps still show the stream as White Brook and the open area as Whitebrook Common. Nowadays, most people call both 'Widbrook' but there is still inconsistency. There are two National Trust metal name plates on the Common. One calls it Widbrook, the other Wildbrook!

Whatever it is called, it is a different habitat to the rest of Cookham, though slightly similar to Cockmarsh. An area of flat grassland, usually cropped short by a variety of ruminants, is surrounded by arable areas and of course the brook, with the road to Maidenhead passing through one end. In winter the Common can get nice and boggy and will attract waders and other birds of passage. An early morning visit is essential to catch the overnight trade, especially in spring-time. With careful and regular observation, my friend John Field has amassed an amazing 120 species on and over the Common. John and his wife Betty live at Whitebrook, adjacent to Widbrook Cottage which has also belonged to the family. John's mum was a Hatch, a licensee at the Kings Arms, whilst his father came to Cookham from Nottingham in 1924, eventually establishing a high class butchers shop in Ellington Park which became John's responsibility until he himself retired. John and Betty married in 1953 at which time Whitebrook was built. Throughout all this time, John was a keen ornithologist and recalls the times of Wryneck and Red-backed Shrikes as regular birds in the village. During his 63 years of observation he has witnessed many changes in the area, and fluctuating fortunes for several species of bird. The reduction in orchard capacity has relegated the Wryneck to a rare bird of passage but large numbers of

Mandarin can now be found, particularly when the Thames overflows its banks near the common, when over one hundred of these spectacularly coloured duck may be seen.

Formerly a native of Far Eastern provinces such as Korea and China, this psychedelic wonder was first introduced to these isles around 1745, first breeding in captivity in 1834. However, it was not until the early twentieth century that escaped specimens established breeding colonies and the Berkshire ones have ranked amongst the largest. A tree-nesting duck, they have taken well to nest box schemes such as one organised on the Cliveden bank of the river and so they often pay Cookham a visit. Of the ducks, none is more stunning than the male Mandarin, so complex being their patterning, they defy description. Large baleful eyes are set in creamy-white cheeks and a brown and green stripe stretches up the nape and over the top of the head, which in turn is precursored by a bright red beak with a yellow knib. A rusty-orange beard and crest enwraps the neck like an open scarf, draped over a rich purple-black back and chest. White stripes of ranking bracket buff side panels and the legs are bright orange. To finally set off this dramatic outfit, two huge vertically-held feathers form cinnamon sails upon the wings.

*Mandarin Duck*

To see large groups of such astoundingly colourful birds on the Widbrook flood plains is a sight to remember. They will be accompanied by similar numbers of marbled females which possess light grey heads and cheeks, delicate brown backs and grey-brown wings. With a notable pair of white spectacles, the lady Mandarins fuss around like busy grannies at the food table, but together with their beaus, they are regarded in their homeland as a symbol of married fidelity. Hardly a missable target for the wildfowler, Mandarins prosper nonetheless because their unpalatable taste ensures their worth for the table is negligible. This is to our good fortune as they are indeed Kings and Queens of the Common.

One of John Field's 'Memorable Birding Moments' involves another occasional visitor to the Common, the Redshank. Essentially a coastal species in winter, where up to a million individuals grace our shores to fight for survival between pursuing tides, these boisterous waders often visit such wetlands on their way to breeding areas, many of which are inland. Over-development along the Thames Valley results in fewer sightings nowadays but one's and two's venture out from Summerleaze pits to augment those passing through. The 'Magpie' of the wader family, Redshanks are noisy, active and over-confident birds. In the air, a white rump and matching wing bars singles out this shank from similar species and it invariably calls raucously just prior to landing on a muddy scrape or tussock of grass, or even a fence-post. It was when a brood of young were being escorted past Whitebrook to the feeding area on the common that one of the parents impertinently alighted upon the cottage roof! The bird even waited patiently for John to fetch his camera to capture this display of exhibitionism on film.

*Redshank*

Snipe, Bar-tailed Godwits and Curlew have all been recorded within sight of Whitebrook's windows and even Quail have paid a visit when the grass was tall enough to conceal it. But it is for quantities of birds that Widbrook is perhaps more noted, in particular seasons. The floods spend the drier months concealed in dungeons beneath the ground, but in many a wet January, life is breathed into them and they arise like phantoms to coat the Common with a glistening sheen. Around their edge, large numbers of Crows, Jackdaws and Rooks descend to probe for the earthworms and other subterranean morsels that are forced to the surface. Similarly, huge flocks of gulls join the fray with Herring, Black-headed and Lesser Black-backed species most prominent. Hundreds of Lapwing come from surrounding farmland to enjoy the boggy conditions, which can last two or three weeks after the river level has returned to normal. The Mandarin are joined by Mallards, Tufted Duck and Coot and for a while, the Common resembles a bird reserve. Plans are afoot to create a man-made trench running parallel to the main river to prevent such flooding in years to come. This will be welcomed by the householders who have moved into the flood plains, but it will perhaps be a pity not to see this almost annual carnival on the Common.

At other times throughout the winter, the Common is a favourite gathering place for flocks of winter thrushes. Every year, Fieldfares and Redwings stream into our country in search of warmer climes and more abundant food. Most originate from Scandinavia, the main departure coinciding with the last supper of Rowan berries. This being a variable feast, arrival times differ each year and even when in this country, their behaviour is somewhat nomadic, large groups wandering around the countryside in search of wild fruit crops. Although the activity of the two species are independent, they will nonetheless often be seen together. Fieldfares are bulky, Mistle-like bold thrushes, with proud grey heads and prominent white eye stripes. The wings and back are a warm mottled brown and the tail almost black, projecting from a distinct grey rump patch. Their stout yellow and black bill is designed to deal with all manner of fruits, or invertebrates and they will be never busier than when ensconced in an orchard where dropped fruit carpet the ground. The chest is boldly striated with dark brown blotches against a warm orange background and white underparts.

On the Common, they hop and skip along in search of grubs, usually with all flock members facing the same way, so the entire ensemble gradually works its way across the open spaces, something like Cowes on yacht racing day. Although rather forceful in character, they are happy to share a food store with Starlings and the Redwings, but if disturbed, will usually wheel off as a group, leaving the other species to plot their own escape. Once airborne, they keep a greater distance between each other than most other flock species, the gregarious nature of the Fieldfares nevertheless confirmed with much *chacking* between individuals.

*Winter Thrushes*

*"I'm turning left. What are you doing?"*. *"I was thinking of turning right, actually. I'll just see what the next guy's going to do"*. *"Does anyone know where we're going?"*. *"We seem to be following that big noisy one again!"*. Close inspection of a flock will reveal noticeable size variation between individuals, perhaps more so than in any other species, apart from the expected size difference between male and female raptors. Their constant murmurings and sharp conversations continue in the trees

and hedges they occupy in between meals. The group name for thrushes in general is a 'mutation', but for this bird, a 'conference' of Fieldfares seems more appropriate.

The Redwing is a far daintier specimen, more like our Song Thrush. A beautiful sculptured head is panelled by creamy eye-stripes and throat lines and rows of spots run down the chest and underparts. The most striking feature is a chestnut patch on the under-wing which extends onto the side of the bird so it might be admired when at rest. Loaned to us by Scandinavians, Greenlanders and Fins, Redwings roam all over Cookham in winter in varying numbers. They will be seen on Cockmarsh, in paddocks, on open fields and in many gardens. If your garden lacks wild fruits to attract them perhaps collecting Elder berries in autumn, freezing them and then putting them out on the bird table in winter might do the trick. Unlike Fieldfares, Redwings are equally at home on woodland floors foraging amongst the leaf litter. Whilst mostly seen in groups of fifty or so, dramatic gatherings of several thousand are not uncommon. A harbinger of oncoming winter, the plaintive *seep* contact calls will be heard at night from late September onwards as this nocturnal traveller sweeps across the country like a feather duster. Linnaeus, who was one of the first to categorise birds into families, referred to the Redwing as 'the Swedish Nightingale' and I have been fortunate enough to hear a little of its song in the unlikely setting of a wintry Quarry Wood. Normally, the Redwings hold concert in flocks of fifty to one hundred individuals and this sound is perfectly matched to the brisk, stark surroundings of woodland in winter. All the birds participate in a complex confabulation, as if trying to out-squawk the next, until it is time to settle down for the night. But the song itself is a buttery confluence of descending trills and Starling-like chatterings, strident yet dainty; powerful then tender. It has a mellow character and, in this Cookham woodland, hundreds of miles from its true haven, I believe it actually sounded home-sick!

The Redwing is the locust of the bird world; advancing inexorably from east to west across our green and pleasant land, thousands upon thousands of them systematically strip every hawthorn hedge, cotoneaster and rowan they can find. From huge flocks of many thousands that reach our shores in favourable wintry gales, they form smaller groups that set off Wales-ward on foraying parties, bent upon the destruction of any and every berry-bearing bush. A flock of fifty or so will de-berry one hundred feet of hawthorn hedge in less than a week. For days on end, there will be the excitement of seeing them in your vicinity in their prim and noble plumage, but when the last morsel of fruit is ceremoniously disposed of in front of the entire raiding party, they will forsake your patch without even a backward glance or a 'thank you very much' and press on to pastures new. Like spilt milk, they slowly diffuse across the nation, the berry line receding like heather in the face of fire. This is unfortunate for its distant cousin, the Waxwing. Far less common as a winter visitor, the Waxwing occasionally erupts into Britain in late winter, only to find most of its prospective dinners consumed by the ravaging Redwings that preceded them. Consequently, it is a rare moment indeed to find a Waxwing feeding in our locale.

Other birds that gather on the Common in fair numbers from late summer onwards are Crows and Rooks. It used to be said that the way to differentiate between these two species was that a Rook on its own was a Crow and Crows in groups were Rooks. This seems a flawed lore of late as Carrion Crows are equally likely to fashion a flock as the Rook, and both will mix together in a feeding frenzy.

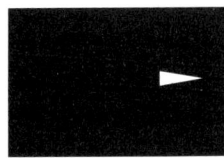
*Rook at Night*

*Crow at Night*

The Rook is discerned by its baggy black trousers, a prominent forehead and a light grey face-patch at the base of a long pointed bill. The Crow has an all-black beak, stouter in form than the Rooks, and lacks the leg feathering too. Rooks breed in close-knit communities and are nesting at the very turn of each new year, their clamourings creating a cacophony of noise as they raid each other's nests for material. Foraging parties span out to a number of preferred fields and meadows to search for leatherjackets and the like to feed to ravenous young (or should that be Raven-ous?). In winter too, Rooks range widely from the rookeries to feeding points which may be grasslands or ploughed fields. There are no Rookeries in Cookham nowadays but Widbrook is a favoured feeding and loafing area so significant numbers can be seen. Carrion Crows breed in small numbers in Cookham but many others use the Common and the fields over towards Cannon Court for dinner parties.

Together, these corvids may seem dull and dowdy, waddling aimlessly around open fields, transporting themselves without obvious purpose from one end of the parish to the other, cawing disconsolately at us lesser beings down below, and bickering with their peers. However, there is another side to these shadowy disputants that is occasionally evidenced in an aerial ballet performed on a warm autumn day when thermals are spiralling up to the heavens. Several hundred Rooks, Crows and Jackdaws will seek out one of these thermals and rise on ethereal elevators to a height of perhaps a thousand feet, soaring on open wings to gain the pinnacle of the warm air column. As each group of birds attain the desired platform, and having sampled the panoramic view from this heady altitude, they spill out of the thermal and commence an exaggerated and heart-stopping descent, twisting and turning, spinning and spiralling, one instant alone, the next in harmony with an adjacent spirit. Urged on by the exhilaration of the moment, they plunge head-first towards the ground and, just when impact seemed inevitable, a quick flick of their broad wings and they are righted once more. Following a brief respite on an adjacent perch, they may again launch themselves onto the escalator and repeat the episode with even greater aplomb. Not a daily occurrence by any means, and perhaps more likely over the ridge of the Dean than over Cockmarsh itself, but a fascinating sequence which defies all thought that life holds no joy for these erstwhile cumbersome creatures.

In his time, John has carried out much study of the birdlife in the area. In 1947, together with wife Betty and Peter Marler, he formed the Slough Natural History Society, specifically to record bird movements in and around the newly-established sewage farm a few miles from Cookham. Some time later, this group became the well-known Middle Thames Natural History Society which studied the fauna and flora of this picturesque sector of the country until 1987. Another Cookham villager active in avian observation and known to John was Mr Edmund Giles. Mr Giles was a food officer and eventually moved to Rye in the late 40's, but whilst in the village, he greatly enjoyed monitoring the fortunes of Red Backed Shrikes and Nightjars in the area. He noted a perceptible increase in breeding Shrike in 1931 and went on to record them until 1945. During that time, he also carefully observed 10 pairs of breeding Wryneck, and up to 10 Wood Warbler nests in the Dean. Cookham Dean Common was a favourite haunt of his, producing visits from Great Grey Shrike, Rough Legged Buzzard, Hen Harrier and Jack Snipe, together with breeding Woodcock. Oh, for a return of those days, as none of these species could realistically be expected there now.

Back on Widbrook, John Field has encountered some unusual species in his time. More than once, passage Quail have let him in on the secret of their presence whilst in August 1947, he found a Corncrake, unfortunately dead beneath telegraph wires. He has observed Curlew and Golden Plover there, but probably his most marked 'Memorable Birding Moment' occurred in June 1970 when, whilst watching Swifts feeding ahead of a thunder storm, a Manx Shearwater flew over the house and westwards over the common. Normally an off-shore species, it is extremely rare to see them inland. He recalls too how much more common Cuckoos used to be in the area, and remembers on one springtime occasion counting no less than 7 over a crop of kale behind the cottage.

*Ring-necked Parakeets*

Another strange sight, and sound over the Common in more recent years is slowly becoming more familiar. Imagine a welcoming stroll from Strand Water over to the Common on a warm, balmy evening, or fresh spring morning. The lofted churtling of the Skylark competes for your ear with the gentle buzz of passing bees on their honey highway. The dried undergrowth rustles briefly as small mice quickly make for their den on your approach. Hedgeways hum with unseen life and the tranquillity of the occasion is absorbed into ones spirit. Suddenly, the sky itself seems to open, as a series of deafening, shrill shrieks pierce the air. The unsettling cry seem omni-directional, coming from every quarter. Just as the ear drum has dampened down this strident vibration, another call, and then another. Like some aerial banshee, defying anything to get in its way, a devilish green dart swoops overhead, screeching its curses incessantly, followed by several of its kind. Where is it? What is it? Will it ever stop? Is this the end of the world? Well, not quite! You will have come across a group of Cookham's latest residents - the Ring-necked Parakeet.

This tropical bird of Oriental origins was first recorded in the wild only as recently as 1969, probably having escaped from a collection. In the short time since then, the national population has grown to an estimated 10,000. Most of them reside in the Thames Valley region, with up to 800 roosting regularly at a recreation centre near Walton, and still more occupying the grounds of Osterley House. Both male and female are striking green parakeets, with very long tails and rosy red bills. Only the male has the narrow collar around its neck which gives the species its name. Gradually, they have spread out along the Thames and its tributaries, inevitably finding the allure of Cookham too much to resist, taking particular interest in the poplars near the Common. Groups of four or six are common, but my friend Peter Gaines has seen as many as 22 together. They are gregarious birds, nesting in small colonies, creating their cradle in tree holes where the female is responsible for incubating the three or four eggs. Constantly active and extremely noisy birds, they have the habits of a gamin and look quite incongruous in our rural setting, but we had best get used to them; they are likely to be here for some time!

The fields surrounding the Common are a refuge for Grey and Red-legged Partridge, Lapwing, Meadow Pipits and Skylarks. Yellowhammers and occasional Corn Bunting may be found. Overhead, other species fly past from the adjacent gravel pit, including Common Tern, Cormorant and various types of gull and duck. Hobby, Kestrel and Sparrow Hawk are regular visitors and I have seen a Buzzard feeding on the ground here on one occasion. Whatever it continues to be called, this remains one of my favourite walks.

*Cormorants*

# In Conclusion

THROUGH THESE PAGES the reader will hopefully have uncovered new-found wonders of this place in which we live. Could it be that the local birds coming into your garden are entreating you to follow them out to meet their friends and relatives beyond? Much awaits to be discovered along the woodland walks, the open marshy expanse, the commons and farmland which surrounds us.

And so it can be seen that the Cookhams are indeed a delight in which to spend time investigating its walks and its avian pleasures. It is a place which should not be hurried, lest one overtakes the slower pace of its beauty and its tranquillity. But if one allows the ambience of this pretty corner of Berkshire to control ones exploration, then it might indeed be found that Cookham really is 'a little piece of Heaven here on Earth'.

*Time to wander, time to stare*
*Gaze upon Creator's fare*
*Come, find freedom, rest and care*
*In glorious Cookham, that's my prayer.*

---

DECEMBER
By common decree, brings the year to an end
And hosting a great celebration.
In all nooks and crannies, every hill and each dale,
In this beautiful part of our nation.

Siskins peal a merry tale
Wrens a-churring, so unfrail.
Robins chunter through the gale
In gifts from above, our birds prevail.

## APPENDIX 1

## SHOPS AND BUSINESSES OF THE NINETIES

To help future historians, these pages attempt to record the recent histories of shops and trades in the village, as best as memories of traders and residents serve. Anomalies are apologised for in advance! If errors are noted, and you care to, please advise the author.

### THE VILLAGE

| | | | |
|---|---|---|---|
| Cookham Village Cars | James Edwards | Feb 96 | (used cars) *(previously Popes Lane Car Sales)* |
| Jasmin Tours | James Smith | 1983 | (Travel Agent) *(previously a goldsmith & o Bradley's the bakers after Bromley's)* |
| Crundles | Jane Briggs | Sep 91 | *(previously a residence, earlier the Post Office)* |
| Stratfords Wine Shippers | Paul Stratford | 1986 | *(previously a gift shop and earlier Jack Smith's, the butchers after Day's the butchers)* |
| Contour Kitchens | Paul Francis (closed Sep 96) | 1981 | *(previously The Merry-go-Round toys & The Walnut Tree tea-rooms)* |
| Barnside Motors | Simon Edwards | 1989 | *(previously Remingtons and John Ostrumoff's)* |
| Andre Garet | Constance Ottaway & Andrew Rogers | | |
| The Boutique | Betty Bond | 1974 | (Menswear) *(previously second hand clothes shop)* |
| Kidz Kid | Alison Parry | 1960 | *(previously a pottery shop.)* |
| Cookham Goldsmith | Mr & Mrs Harris | 1994 | |
| Danny's Hairdresser | Danny Woodford | 1972 | *(was a bookshop)* |
| Simply Hair | Salvo Pulsiventi | 1991 | *(used to be the Goldsmiths)* |
| Mary Brooks | Mary Brooks | 1982 | *(used to be Budgens)* |
| Andrew Milsom & Ptnrs | | May 95 | *(was Quadrille gift shop, Mrs Twitchen & Mrs Johnson. Earlier a Budgens)* |
| The Marlow Donkey | Ian Keay | 1994 | (Estate Agents) *(previously Roger Platts)* |
| Libby of the Little Shop | Libby Harrington | 1967 | (Model Railways *(previously Lloyds Bank)* |
| The Two Roses | Marion Smith | 1975 | *(previously Tarrystone Café)* |
| Fiorni | Jenny Fiore | 1980 | *(previously two cottages and Steamer Ticket Office)* |
| Pineneedles | (closed 1995) | | (Pine Furniture) |
| Andre Garet | Kathleen Ottaway | 1980 | (Shoe Boutique) |
| Peking Inn | | 1989 | *(previously Copper Kettle Café)* |
| The B Shop | Betty Bond | 1989 | *(previously an insurance office)* |
| Vicki Bond | Vicki Bond | 1989 | *(previously Hocket & Pocket, caravan repairs)* |
| EXCEL Swimming Pools | (closed 1995) | | |
| Forge Motor Co | John & Edward Knight | 1954 | *(previously the Forge)* |

107

**COOKHAM ARCADE** (built on old International Stores site)

| | | | |
|---|---|---|---|
| Lovely | Cynthia Johnson | Oct 95 | (Ladies lingerie) |
| A Touch of Gold | Lothar Schmelter | April 96 | *(was Arcade Antiques, and Georgiou)* |
| Chic Hairdressing | Karen Brice | 1975 | (clothing) *(was already a hairdressers)* |
| Seconds Out | Mr & Mrs Milbourn | 1990 | *(was Model Motors which moved to Bourne End)* |
| Sandra Francis Arts | Sandra Francis | | |
| Pauline's | Darren Jones | 1996 | (newsagent) *(previously same name for 16 years)* |

**THE PARADE**

| | | | |
|---|---|---|---|
| CIC Insurance | | July 94 | *(previously Westminster Bank)* |
| Nationwide Building Soc | | 1978 | *(previously Miss Smither hairdresser & wool shop)* |
| Clippers (hairdresser) | Brent Wood | 1975 | *(previously Pool's hardware shop)* |
| Bentley's Dry Cleaners | Ragen Family | Aug 93 | *(previously Waterman estate agents)* |
| Village Hardware | Fred Haines | July 93 | *(previously Church's hardware shop, a Ski shop & a horse tackle shop)* |
| St Anne's House | Robin Denville | 1983 | Dental Practice *(previously antique shop and graphic design business)* |
| The Village Countrystore | Darren Jones | | *(previously Groves newsagents which burnt down, & Websters Coal & Corn)* |
| Reliance Shoe Repairs | Jeremiah Stokes | 1962 | *(previously Ackrills & Sayles Newsagents)* |
| Maidenhead Bait & Tackle | M J Hutt | Nov 94 | *(previously Poole's Electrical and before that a laundrette)* |
| Hutt Refrigeration | M J Hutt | Nov 94 | " " |
| Clothes Care | Mr Thompson | 1989 | *(previously Harrold's wool shop, earlier a Sketchley's Dry Cleaner)* |
| Alfonso's Restaurant | Alfonso | Dec 83 | *(was previously a French Restaurant)* |
| Michael Hairdresser | Michael Weinblatt | 1978 | *(was already a hairdresser)* |
| Cookham Racing Service | Ken Wilkes | Feb 93 | *(previously Fridge/Freezer business and Wavy Line Stores)* |
| Cookham Bakery & Delicatessen | | | *(previously Patsy's Pantry & Langley's Bakery)* |
| The Fruit Bowl | Mr Brimble | 1974 | (until 31/8/96) *(previously a fruit shop. Cookham Antiques, Gary Wallace, Oct 1996)* |
| The Toy Shop | Mr & Mrs Sargeant | 1968 | |
| Chevron Typesetters | Mr Sargeant | | |
| Threshers Off Licence | John Bairstow | 1985 | *(was clothes & haberdashery shop, previously a shoe shop)* |
| Peter Gigg (Butchers) | Peter Gigg | 1969 | |
| Royal Dry Cleaners | R. Solanky | 1994 | |
| B & A Pets | Bob Griffiths | Apr 94 | *(previously Cost Cutters frozen foods & Kentwood)* |
| At Leisure Travel | | | *(previously The Bulb Shop - electrical, and Michael Mann - Accountant)* |
| D & W Autos | Pete Dutfield | c1976 | |

108

## THE LOWER ROAD

| | | | |
|---|---|---|---|
| The Post Office | | | |
| Cookham Florist | Margaret Murphy | 1993 | *(previously Gardener's florist, Gallagher's hairdresser & Lloyds Bank)* |
| Fine Signs | Roger Fortescue | | *(previously Shackels, the laundry)* |
| Pike Smith & Kemp | (Estate Agents) | 1990 | *(previously Hamptons) Thistle Cottage* |
| Country Stoves | Martin Jarvis | Nov 79 | *(previously florist & green-grocers)* |
| Keith Macey (meats) | Keith Macey | 1986 | *(previously Paul Cowan, butcher, & his father before him)* |
| Europower Management | Mr & Mrs Boakes | 1989 | *(previously Spillet & Tomlins Wavy Line greengrocers)* |
| Intopia | Vicki Read | Nov 96 | *(previously Deacon Read interior decorator, & Hedger's bookshop)* |
| Hair Flair | Wendy Steeden | 1965 | *(previously an electrical store)* |
| Car Parts (Cookham) | Richard Burfoot | 1990 | *(previously car accessories and cycle shop & Mrs Lake's haberdashery)* |
| Seconds Out (clothing) | David Milburn | 1985 | *(previously Dietreich Pet Shop & Dixon's grocery)* |
| GKL Communications | (Advertising & Marketing) | Dec 85 | *(previously Rise Autos)* |
| The Pharmacy | G & N Brunsden | 1930 | *(previously Mr Brunsden's father)* |
| Home & Garden | Pauline Madden | 1995 | *(previously shop of same name owned by sisters Joan and Barbara Bedwell)* |
| Colin Hatch | (Builders) | | |

## THE DEAN

| | | | |
|---|---|---|---|
| The Post Office | Sam & Rhonda Surman | 1987 | *(converted to PO by Chris Kinge 1960)* |
| Aristocuts (Hairdressers) | Margaret Foster | 1984 | *(was Claudette's, and Howlett's Grocery & Robinsons)* |
| Sawfords Classics & Sports | Rolls Family | 1993 | *(empty 2 years, previously: Suburu Dealer, Mr Breuer & earlier, a School)* |
| Henderson's Garage | Henderson Family | Apr 93 | *Also "Autoshine". (previously Dean Farm Garage)* |
| The Forge | David Matthews | | |

## ELSEWHERE

| | | | |
|---|---|---|---|
| Anglewest Ltd | | 1993 | Peace Lane (Scaffolding) |
| Simon Hall Ass | Simon Hall | 1978 | Halldore Hill (Marketing & Advertising) |
| Welbon Haskell | Jonathan Haskell | 1982 | *(since 1900, coal merchant, dry cleaners, hairdressers, grocery, chiropodists, & antiques)* |
| Samrai Foodstores | Samrai Family | Nov 85 | Whyteladyes Lane *(previously Abraham's Stores)* |
| Hillcrest Stores | Mrs Brar | c 1960 | |
| Woottens Boatyard | Patrick Wootten | 1908 | (Restoration) *(Father and Grandfather before him)* |

There have been many shops and traders lost to the village in recent years due to the competition of larger supermarkets in the area; a lesson to us to remember to support our local shops if we do not want to lose the advantages they provide us and their role in maintaining village life.

## APPENDIX 2

# BIBLIOGRAPHY

| | |
|---|---|
| Adventures Among Birds | W H Hudson |
| Alice Ray Morton's Cookham | Roger Parkes |
| All the Birds of the Bible | Alice Parmelee |
| Berkshire Bird Bulletin (produced monthly) | B D Clews et al |
| Berkshire County Ornithological Records | Various Authors - (1915 to 1995) |
| Birds In A Village | W H Hudson |
| Birds of Berkshire & Buckinghamshire | Alexander W M Clark Kennedy |
| Sweet Thames Run Softly | Robert Gibbings |
| The Atlas of Breeding Birds of Britain | Peter Lack |
| The Birds of Buckinghamshire & East Berkshire | A C Fraser & R E Youngman |
| The Story of Cookham | Robin and Val Bootle |
| The Wildlife of the Thames Counties | Richard Fitter |
| Victorian County History of Berkshire | Noble (1906) |
| Where to Watch Birds in Berkshire etc. | B D Clews, P Trodd, A Heryet |

APPENDIX 3

# GLOSSARY & LIST OF ILLUSTRATIONS

## GLOSSARY

| | | | | | | |
|---|---|---|---|---|---|---|
| Bins | = | Binoculars | Ternery | = | Tern Colony |
| Spug | = | Sparrow | Passerine | = | Song Bird |
| Shivoo | = | Party | Lamberts | = | Units of Light |
| Rill | = | Brook | | | |

## ILLUSTRATIONS

**Photographs**
 Quarry Hotel & Aircraft, loaned by **David Wright**
 Rev David Rossdale **Parish Centre**
 Remainder **Brian Clews**

**Drawings**
 Cover Line Drawing **David Colthup**
 Coloured Cover Drawings **Barbara Clews**
 Elizabeth House & Old Farm House **David Wright**
 Pied Wagtail **Barbara Clews**
 The Following Birds: **A P Chick**
  Spotted Flycatcher, Tufted Duck, Hobby,
  Sand Martin & Swallow, Goldfinch, Dabchick,
  Mandarin, Cormorant
 The Following Drawings: **Barbara Pritchard**
  Tawny Owl, Long Tailed Tit, Lapwing, Pheasant,
  Moorhen, Heron, Kingfisher, Fieldmouse, Kestrel,
  Reed Bunting, Tawny Young, Wren, Swans,
  Barn Owl, Robin, Redwing & Fieldfares
 All others **Brian Clews**

**Poetry & Writings**
 Historic Quotations & Poetry **Writers named in text**
 Other Poetry **Brian Clews**
 Scriptures **The Holy Bible**

# LIST OF SUBSCRIBERS

Martin & Shirley Gostling
Fredk. J. Thacker & Patricia Thacker *(died 29.5.96)*
Ramon & Kathie Whiddett
Roger & Tessa Parkes
Dr. Caleb W. Davies CMG & Mrs Joan Davies
John & Sue Ferguson
Paul, Judy, Adriana Renucci
Jennifer Fiore (Fiorini)
Mary & Fernand Roofthooft
Peter & Veronica Moran
Len & Pauline Sheppard
Viv & Marilyn Elstow
Gladys & Michael Snoding
Cookham Rise Primary School
Stephen, Rosie Smith & Lorraine Kelly Smith
Bert, Gwen, Betty Dodd
Mervyn & Allison Dodd
Mr & Mrs G.W. Dodd
Timmy, Lynda, Billy Mallett
Steve, Kim, Emily, Lewis & baby Green
Paul, Jacquie, Joshua Rollett
Jenny, Roger, Susie & Michele Harris
John, Anne, Robert Coomber
Peter & Julie Winyard

Julie, Robert, James & Zoe Overall
Mr & Mrs Peter Fisher
Diane & Stuart Large
Peter, Sue & Christopher Turner
Rachel & Uel Magowan
Alan & Ellen Common
James & Joanna Reece
John, Jane, Dominique, David, Kate, & Stephanie Belton
Pam & Dr. Ennis Giordani
Elizabeth, Stephen & Jane Runnacles
Han, Irma, Ron & Sophie Kieftenbeld
Dr. Mahmood & Mrs Tracey Suleiman
Arif & Riya Suleiman
Quentin & Julia Jarman
Gillian Hague, Christopher, Jeremy & Ian Batt
Ben, Rory & Clara Millar
Johanna & Paul Layng
David & Estelle Cornwell
Margaret & Tony Johnston
Robert & Jean Stockhausen
Simon & Sheila Sturge

Paul, Shanni, & Lucienne Spencer
John Michael & Christina Adie Serls
Jim & Marion Wiggins
Nigel & Elisabeth Sanders
Bill, Christopher & Stephen Meads
Joanna & Marcia Shuttleworth
Peter, Maureen, Rachel, Robert & Lyndsey Turvey
Air Marshal Sir Patrick & Lady Dunn
Brian, Joan & Rebecca Swatton
Corrine & David Spice
Jo, Peter, Janet, Hannah, & Christopher Dutfield
Michael Brian & Sheila Yvonne West
Christine & Alan Skudder
Alan, Maureen, Caroline & Richard Reid
Deborah & Shekeila Palmer
Susan, Richard & Sara Poad
Denham & Lesley Gilbart-Smith

Alistair John & Nicola Jane Eglinton
Hayley & Samantha Cox
Robin, Chrissie, Charlotte, Alice & Bethany Simons-Denville
Neville & Ian Keay
Charles & Marion Elly
Libby Harrington,
Margaret Wells & staff of Libby of The Little Shop
Michael Cameron-Wood
Jeremy & Tina Langham
Artscape Gardening
Stephen Archibald
Nicholas Corble
Bernadette & Derek Clarke
Peter, Carol, Holly & Sacha Evans
Karen & Nigel Rivers
Dorothy, Roger James, Luca
Gariel Piercey; Joellyn & Arendall Edith Branch Piercey
Wendy, Malcolm, Abigail & Adam Roels
Freda & Iolo Hughes
Gurmail, Satwant, Sunita & Jeeven Nagra

## List of subscribers *(continued)*

Simon, Sandra, Louise & Gareth Edwards
Capt. F.J. Turk (MVO) & Mrs. M.C Turk
Sir George & Lady Young
Alison & Jon Sworn
Arthur & Pauline Hancock
Sam & Rhonda Surman
Edna & Norman Taylor
Mr & Mrs. John Chappell
Graham & Frankie Paynter
David & Anne Puddle
Rev. John Copping
Christine & John Fenton
Jack & Mary Taylor
The Greenwood Family
Angela, Brian, Richard & Debra Jones
Angus & Eileen Murray
Bob, Angela, Catherine, Sarah Griffiths & Joan Hill
Roy & Jean Thompson
Beryl, Gordon, Paula, Giles & Joanna Batten
Michael T, Sally M. & Robert T. Moore
Barry & Christine Frewing
B.S & L.M.V Hamilton
Dr. & Mrs Vaudrey Mercer

Drs. David & Julia Mercer
Major T.L. Wilson-Jerrim MC
Barbara & David Pritchard
Keith, Jacqueline, Benjamin & Christopher Johnson
Tom, Charlotte & William Quelch
Colin, Maggie, Jenny, Lucy & Buddy (the dog) Hyndman
Penny, Crispin & Elliott Herrod-Taylor
Stuart & Heather Conlin
Peter & Annette Rogers
Mitch, Cary, Kate, Bethan, & Annie-Ruth Holyoake
Amor & Robert Humphrey
Andy Cooper & Val Lyness
John, Sally, Rupert, Sarah & Georgina Lloyd-Parry
Tricia, Amy, Danielle, Jean & Samantha Phillips
Denis & Judy Wright
Douglas & Maureen Talintyre
Vyvyan, Pam, Gareth & Rebekah Rees
David & Pamela Fuller
Howard, Mary & Lucy Martin

Ruth Hoskin & Andy Strowbridge
Marcela & Brad Wilson
Philip & Dorothy Wilder
Eddie Smyth & Family
Eric, Susan, Paul, Sarah, John, & Mark Mason
Jonathan, Ceri & Jordan Davies
Peter & Valerie Sargster
Vernon, Elizabeth, James, Angela, Mark & William Sankey
Alec & Dorothy Gardner-Medwin
Nancy & Frances Harvey
Patrick & Prunella Davey
Major & Mrs. S.G.D. Fenton
Jo & Andrew Speakman
Clair Elizabeth & Lawrence William Hunt
The Sawyer Family
Peter John & Jill Frances Finlan
John, Anica, Helen & Mark Wilkinson
Colin & Brenda Timberlake
Richard & Joanna Hannam
Peter & Rebecca Barker

Stanley F & Georgina D. Jones
Stanley & Margaret Walter
John, Ann, Neal, Matthew & James Gibbings
Robert John & Geoffrey Nigel Sands
Walter (Mick) Groves
Hugh & Joan Somerville
John & Mary Hotchkiss
Michael, Suzanne, Michelle & Christopher Price
Phillip, Deborah & James Ruck
Susan & Drew Mason
Mike & Ann Bossingham
Roger & Judith White
Susan & Michael Mather
Robert, Pauline, Ross, Justin, & Monica Mandeville
John, Margaret & Jane Tinker
Sheila A Copas-Groves
Miss April E. Groves
Cookham Dean PrimarySchool
Adrian, Oliver, & Hazel Sharpe
Catherine Lesley & Sarah Victoria Allerton

## List of subscribers (continued)

| | | |
|---|---|---|
| David & Marie-Paule Nicholas | Barbara Clews | Liz Kwantes | Kaye Menzies |
| H.G & Mrs. M.C. Amon | David & Sue Wright | Sam Woods | Mary & Jim Haines |
| A.M & A.L. Clements | Sidney Jewell | Dot & Andy Croall | Jean L. Little |
| Roderick, Susan, Catherine, & Joyce Gauld | Dennis Percy Gale | Stan & Jean Sexton | Mrs E.L. White |
| Bob, Ruth, Mandi & Jeremy Deacon | Jenny Jerrum | The Gurney Family | Mrs E.A. Gradon |
| Maureen & Phillipa Hudson | John Shaw | Mr. & Mrs. J Walker | Mrs. B. Tomlin |
| David & Heather Bateson | Philip & Sue Bryant | Pat & Simon Davis | Mrs. W. Hull |
| J.W, H.B, C.J, J.S &N.J.U Edwards | Pamela Tisdale | Paul & Jack Ovens | John & Betty Field |
| Paul, Jane, Peter, Sophie, Anna & Oliver Narizzano | Mark Gannon | Ann & Dennis Oliver | H. Booth |
| Mr & Mrs. T. Deadman | Mrs. Trodd | Keith Thompson | Mary Davis |
| Susan & Sharon Deadman | Mavis Ratcliffe | Eric & Olive Rogers | Linda Heyes |
| Pete, Sue & Alex Lale | Edna Harris | Peter & Eva Bishop | Mrs. Iris S. Jones |
| D, E H, T D & A W Mileham | M.J. Lewis | Brian & Dot Parker | Brian B. Long |
| Mr. & Mrs. P. Langton | Jim & Alison Peck | Ruth & Derek Carver | Terry Wild |
| Maureen& Charles Wingrove | Mrs. A.J. Peters | Jack Randell | AJ & JM Evans |
| Alison Jane Poynter | Mary Ellis | Audrey Sale | Laura Vohryzek |
| Mark Poynter | Miss C.L. Jones | Terry Mosdell | Paul Samuel |
| L. & D. Whitworth | Mrs. K. Langton | Roy & Diana Belcher | David A. Hawkins |
| David Rossdale | David Austen | Betty Bond | Major R.L.J. Pott |
| Wendy Craig | Cheri Gane | Anne Keating | Paul Connor |
| Doll & Claire Cooper | Michael Cooper | Chris & Jane Helm | Pat & Barrie Taylor |
| Betty Perfect | Roy & Norma Gigg | Phyllis Middleton | Lesley Aston |
| | Brenda Miller | Tim Twitchen | Marta Makowska |
| | Judy & Norman Lane | Graham Wray | Colin Jones |
| | Eleanor Cooney | Kim & Barry Hobbs | Alan Finch |
| | Judy Jones | Inge & Tony Beck | Simon & Janet Elvin |
| | Mr. T. Hughes | Peter & Irene Gaines | David Moore |
| | Patrick & Sonia Bell | E.T. Schiff | Mrs. Janet Mobbs |
| | The Ferris Family | Fiona & Douglas Bay | J. Kit Cuthbert |

## List of subscribers (continued)

E.R & I.A Rutland
Margaret Cragg
Mrs. D. Scotford
Mary K. McQuade
Avril & Peter Lowe
M.J & C.V Thorne
B.J & J Cutler
Herries School
Neil Baldry
Laura & Ron Ayers
John & Ruth Bowley
Vera Fletcher
John & Bridie Webb
Kath & Ron Blackall
Marsali Poore
Brian Hicks
Jim Parsons
Nick Johnson
George Perczel
Hedley & June Bray
Philip Bray
S. B. A & T. Wray
L. Fulker
P. Anderson
C. Ellis
M. Gabb
Celia Macey
Mrs Irene Self
Marion Edkins

Joyce Vaughan
Dorothy Fee
The Odney Club
Linda Stroud
Josie & Nigel Lemon
Susan L. Gales
Janet & John Owen
Sandy Higgs
Janet Cooper
Malcolm Wilkes
D.J. Colthup
John Clews
Kathleen Ruth Kent
Harman & Joan Dean
Mr. A.F. Harris
Bill & Avril Edge
M & H Brodie
Nora Lumsden
Nicolas Lindley
Jillian Fraser
Nola & David Edgar
Toni Purnell
T.J. & B.A. Ward
Eric & Hazel Collins
Lizzie Wears
Mr. C.R. Merton
Bob Benwell
Joy Campbell
Roger Wells

L & J Boothman
Brenda Rutland
Pamela & Brian Edwards
Patricia & John Graham
Christine Higgins
Fred & Cal Haigh
Felicity, Alexander, James
  & Joanne Haigh
Colin Albert Helmuth &
  Lynda May Daniel
Tord & Elaine Norstrom
Richard Webb
Mark Turner
Helen Sedgwick
Kerrie Stevens
Steve & Andrea Barron
Peter, Carol, Suzanna &
  Christopher Knight
Alastair, Suzanne, Michelle
  & Peter Watt
Mary Ollett
Monica J. Taylor
John & Kathryn Rickman
A.M.R. Loveday
Pamela & Louisa Knight
Arthur & Mildred White
Phillippa Boyland
Dora Hodge

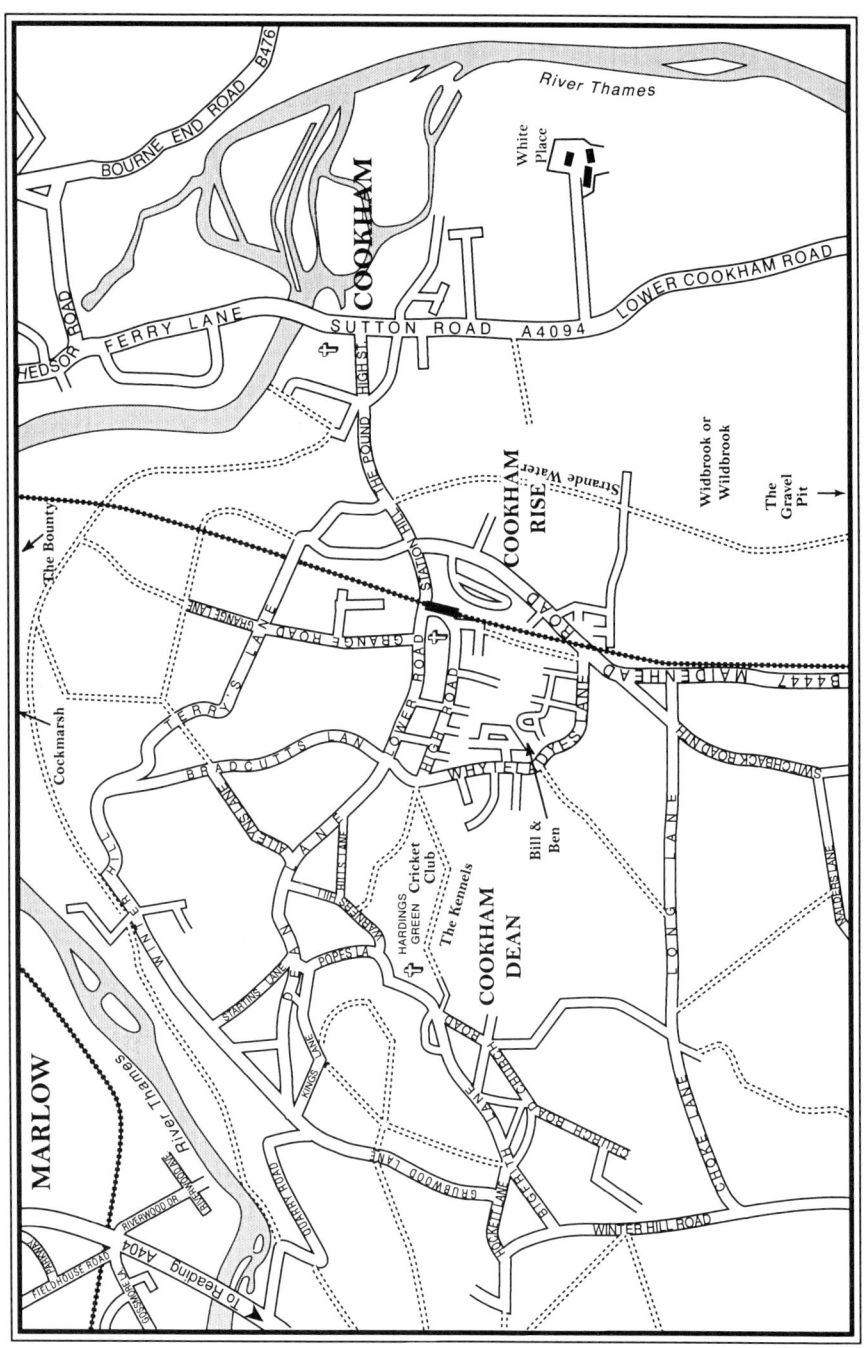

Alleyns Lane

Sawfords Garage – The Dean

The Rise from The Dean

Lower Road

Royal Cottages – The Dean

Cookham Dean War Memorial

*The Crown*                                              *The Anchor*

*Holy Trinity*                                       *The Village War Memorial*

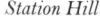

*Station Hill*                                            *Moor Hall*